The Wise Owl Guide to ...

DANTES Subject Standardized Test (DSST)

Organizational Behavior

Printed in the United States of America

ISBN-10: 1470075865
ISBN-13: 9781470075866
Library of Congress Control Number: 2012933274

[redacted]

Table of Contents

Introduction

Are you going to learn everything about organizational behavior in this study guide? Certainly not! But… are you going to learn enough to pass the DSST test? Yes! The DSST (Dantes Subject Standardized Test) series covers the most common topics in a traditional college course. This book is written in a format that is easy-to-read, understand and remember. Organizational behavior is a relevant real-world topic, and no matter if you have a test to pass or not this information will make you feel like a more educated person for knowing it.

About the Test

The exam (and this book) covers topics such as:

- Organizational behavior overview
- Individual processes and characteristics
- Interpersonal and group processes and characteristics
- Organizational processes and characteristics
- Change and development processes

This test guide includes a 100-question practice test to ensure a solid handle on the course information.

PART I ORGANIZATIONAL BEHAVIOR OVERVIEW

This test is divided among many areas of organizational behavior. This portion of the test will account for approximately six percent of the test questions. Part I will cover:

- The field of organizational behavior
- The study of organizational behavior

THE FIELD OF ORGANIZATIONAL BEHAVIOR

Organizational behavior (OB) is an interdisciplinary applied science of the study of people and their behavior in an organization. OB uses psychology, management, sociology, organizational theory, social psychology, statistics, political science, information technology, counseling, stress management, ethics and more. OB examines many behaviors that include; individuals, interpersonal, group, intergroup and whole system. OB seeks to describe, understand, predict and control behavior. Four key forces affect organizations today:

- People (individuals and groups)
- Structure (jobs and relationships)
- Technology (information technology and machinery)
- Environment (government, competition and society)

Organizational systems consist of:

- **Vision** – desired future state
- **Mission** – purpose
- **Goals** – specific hopeful achievements in a time period

The four functions of management are:

- **Planning** – recognition of goals and strategies
- **Organizing** – roles and choosing an organizational fit
- **Leading** – influencing and inspiring followers
- **Controlling** – ensuring organization is on track

HISTORY OF ORGANIZATIONAL BEHAVIOR

Three significant movements shaped today's OB:

- **Human relations movement**
    - Hawthorne – recent tests reveal data from the Hawthorne experiments are invalid, main variables of the experiment were based on fear of unemployment and the Great Depression.

- Mayo and Follett's *The Human Problems of an Industrial Civilization* (1933) advised management to motivate through employees emotional needs.
- McGregor's *The Human Side of Enterprise* (1960) outlined two contrasting views: Theory X (people dislike work) and Theory Y (people like work):
  - **Theory X** assumes most people dislike work, have little ambition and appreciate security. Overall, employees require control, threats and punishment.
  - **Theory Y** assumes most people find work natural, engage in self-direction and have potential to be great. Overall, employees require development to reach their potential and help to realize common rewards.

- **Total quality management (TQM) movement** – (1980) inspired by documentary *If Japan Can ... Why Can't We?*
  - W. Edwards Deming focused on training, helpful leadership, elimination of fear, process improvements, teamwork and barrier elimination.
  - Four principles of TQM are; do it right the first time, listen and learn from employees and customers, make constant process improvements, and build teamwork and trust.
  - TQM theory is that 85% of failures are due to system issues (rules, machinery or management) and 15% are due to workers failures.
- **Contingency approach movement** – situational vs. set leadership methods.

ORGANIZATIONAL CULTURE

The **organizational culture** is the shared values and beliefs of a cultural identity. It is an independent variable affecting an employee's attitudes and behaviors. The **dominant culture** expresses the core values shared by the majority. There are three layers of organizational culture:

- **Observable artifacts** – includes dress code, awards, myths and stories about the organization
- **Espoused values** – the enduring belief in conduct or end-state which include five key components; beliefs,

desirable end-state, transcend situations, guide selection of behavior and are ordered by importance

  - **Enacted values** – the values that are exhibited in employee behavior, leaders must try to bridge the gap between espoused and enacted values

- **Basic assumptions** – the underlying assumptions that represent the core culture and are highly resistant to change (e.g., Apple's focus on innovation)

Organizational culture is important and serves four main functions:

- **Organizational identity** – pride in being part of a group
- **Collective commitments** – join together and commit to a cause or value (e.g., customer service)
- **Social system stability** – view work as positive and reinforcing
- **Sense-making device** – grasp an organization's choices

Organizational culture has seven primary characteristics:

- Innovation and risk taking
- Attention to detail
- Outcome orientation
- People orientation
- Team orientation
- Aggressiveness
- Stability

Organizational culture is created in three ways:

- Purposeful selection of employees who "fit"
- Indoctrination and socialization, the three stages of socialization are:
  - **Prearrival** – assumption that an employee comes with a set of values, attitudes and expectations
  - **Encounter** – newly hired employee confronts dichotomy between expectations and reality
  - **Metamorphosis** – new member becomes comfortable with the organization
- Role modeling of founders

Strong cultures can substitute formalization. Subcultures tend to develop in large organizations that reflect common problems, situations or experiences. Subcultures are likely defined by geographic or departmental separations. Organizational culture can become a liability when the shared values conflict with effectiveness (e.g., when an organization is undergoing change).

Fundamental Concepts

Two separate natures divide the **fundamental concepts** (enduring principles) of organizational behavior:

- People
  - Law of individual differences (uniqueness)
  - Selective perception
  - Whole person
  - Motivation
  - Drive for self-efficacy
  - Values
- Organizations
  - Social system
  - Mutual interest – understanding that organization's and people rely on each other
  - Organizational ethics
    - **Ethical dilemmas** (all choices are deemed undesirable for potential harmful consequences) the best way to address organizational ethics is to spell it out on paper in a code of ethics, which should be complementary to the company's policies and procedures

Framework

A **paradigm** is a framework of possible explanations for how something may work. There are four basic models of organizational behavior:

- **Autocratic** – power and authority to achieve objective, with an emphasis on obedience (high human cost)
- **Custodial** – security needs (good benefits) to keep employees (dependency can develop)
  - Dependency fosters **passive cooperation** that is not much more effective than the autocratic model
- **Supportive** – uses leadership to provide a growth climate for the employees, giving the employees participation and task involvement with stronger motivation to work

- **Collegial** – extends the supportive model by giving people a common purpose (requiring teamwork), managers are seen as team-players

The three frameworks of organizational culture are:

- Organizational Culture Inventory
- Competing Values Framework
- Organizational Culture Profile

Developed by Robert Quinn and Kim Cameron, **Competing Values Framework** is the most popular. Managers understand, measure and change organizational culture. Quinn and Cameron developed an assessment instrument to assess between four culture types:

Competing Values Framework

Clan • Collaborative and friendly with leaders in parental roles • Internally focused; values flexibility rather than stability or control	**Adhocracy** • Dynamic work environment; leaders inspire innovation • Externally focused; values flexibility
Hierarchy • Leaders are like coordinators • Internally focused; values stability and control	**Market** • Competitive culture with focus on customer • Externally focused; values stability and control

Figure 1 Competing Values Framework

THE STUDY OF ORGANIZATIONAL BEHAVIOR

OB researches behavioral theories to modify behavior. The four approaches to OB are:

- **Human resources** – employee growth and development
- **Contingency** – leadership behaviors based on situation
- **Results-oriented** – efficiency
- **Systems** – complexity of organizational interrelationships

Commonsense and casual theoretical approaches to human behavior can cause problems; a systematic approach to human behavior predictions is best. **Systematic studies** investigate cause and effect relationships based on scientific evidence with data under controlled conditions evaluated in a thorough manner. A

model is an abstract of reality (a simplification of a real-world phenomenon). There are two variables in scientific evaluation:

- **Dependent variable** – absenteeism, turnover, deviant workplace behaviors, productivity, job satisfaction and organizational citizenship behavior
- **Independent variable** – stands alone and is not changed by other variables (e.g., age of employee)

Conclusions emerge from analysis of the data. Conclusions in OB can find ways to modify dependent variables. Understanding employee abilities and biographical characteristics can help predict organizational performance:

- Employees abilities (e.g., mental, physical capacities)
- Biographical characteristics (e.g., age, gender, race)
    - Assumptions that older workers are not as productive are disproven, studies show older workers exhibit high levels of judgment, are less likely to leave, have a strong work ethic and are committed to quality
    - Some assumed gender differences (e.g., problem-solving, analytical skills) are not true, but working mothers are more likely to want part-time work, flexible scheduling and/or telecommuting
    - Race issues crop up with a bias for individuals to favor those of their own race for performance evaluations, promotions and pay raises
    - Employees with tenure are generally more productive and experience fewer absences

Part II Individual processes and characteristics

This test is divided among many areas of organizational behavior. This portion of the test will account for approximately 36 percent of the test questions. Part II will cover:

- Perceptual processes
- Personality
- Attitudes
- Learning processes
- Motivation
- Work stress and the individual

Perceptual processes

The **perceptual process** is how a person interprets their environment. The social information-processing model involves a four-stage information processing sequence:

- Stage one – comprehension
    - Conscious awareness, something that is different or accompanies a benefit or punishment gets the most attention (**salient**)
- Stage two – encoding and simplification
    - Information is translated for storing in to memory through categorization of objects and schema, stereotypes of an object are usually used during the encoding process
- Stage three – storage and retention
    - Moving the information to long-term memory (in one of three categories) event memory, semantic memory (general knowledge) or person memory
- Stage four – retrieval and response
    - Used for judgments and decisions

Managers use perceptions for a wide range of activities including hiring, performance appraisals, leadership, communication and influence. Barriers to perception include:

- **Selective perception** – processing only information that aligns with existing beliefs (only see what we want to see)
- **Halo effect** – taking a single characteristic and forming a general impression (e.g., promotion because attractive)

- **Contrast effects** – reaction based on comparison to others (e.g., good skills compared to great skills may reflect poorly on the one with good skills)
- **Projection** – seeing self in someone else
- **Stereotyping** – general determination of a person based on preconceived notions of a group they belong to

ATTRIBUTIONAL APPROACHES TO PERCEPTION AND BEHAVIOR

Attribution theory is the idea that people try to examine causes of behavior. **Causal attributions** are the inferred causes of behavior. Fritz Heider was the founder of attribution theory proposing that behavior comes from within (e.g., ability) or from the environment (e.g., task complexity). Harold Kelley took Heider's work further by trying to identify the major attributions, believing people make causal attributions after gathering information about three major behaviors:

- **Consensus** – comparing behavior with peers
    - High consensus is when one acts like the rest of the group, low is when they act differently
- **Distinctiveness** – comparing behavior on one task with behavior on other tasks (if a person has different behaviors in different situations)
    - High distinctiveness means person performs task differently than they perform other tasks, low distinctiveness means stable performance
- **Consistency** – judging performance of a task over time
    - High consistency indicates the task is performed the same over time, low means that the task is performed unstably

Two major attribution tendencies that distort ones perception of others are the fundamental attribution bias and the self-serving bias. The **fundamental attribution bias** ignores environmental factors that impact behavior. The **self-serving bias** is the tendency to take more credit for successes than failures.

PERSONALITY

Personality is the combination of relatively stable physical and mental characteristics. Personality is derived from genetics and environments. There are five basic dimensions of personality (Big Five personality dimensions):

- **Extraversion** (outgoing and sociable)
- **Agreeableness** (trusting and good-natured)
- **Conscientiousness** (responsible and dependable)
- **Emotional stability** (relaxed and unworried)
- **Openness to experiences** (imaginative and broad-minded)

In general, conscientiousness is the closest linked to positive job performance, while extraversion is associated to the best salespeople and managers. The **proactive personality** is someone who scores high on conscientiousness, shows initiative and seeks to change the status quo for the better.

Personality assessments

Assessment tools measure the strength of personalities. The most widely used one is Myer-Briggs Type Indicator (MBTI). The **MBTI** classifies people as:

- Extroverts or introverts
- Sensing or intuitive
- Thinking or feeling
- Judging or perceiving

The MBTI is not a strong indicator of job performance, but useful for increased self-awareness and career guidance.

Major traits affecting OB

The major personality traits that effect OB are:

- **Core self-evaluation** –self-like and viewed effectiveness
- **Machiavellianism** – pragmatism, emotional distance, manipulation and belief that ends justify means (useful in a job focused on "winning")
- **Narcissism** – sense of self-importance, excessive self-admiration, entitlement and arrogance
- **Self-monitoring** – adjust behavior to fit a situation
- **Risk taking** – willingness to take chances (high-risk takers make rapid decisions with less information) the need for risk takers depends on nature of the organization
- **Type A or Type B** – Type As are aggressive and try to achieve more and more, while Type B's are less stressed
- **Proactive** – not afraid to buck convention, engage in civic behavior and voice opinions (useful change agents)

Locus of control

A person's **locus of control** is the degree in which a person believes they control their destiny. There are two types:

- **Internal** – things happen due to self-actions
    - More ethical, greater motivation, higher expectations, better performance, more satisfied with jobs and higher pay
- **External** – things happen due to luck or chance
    - Limited accountability for self-actions and anxious

Attitudes

An **attitude** is a relatively stable learned predisposition toward specific objects, persons or situations. Typically, values and attitudes agree. There are three main components of an attitude:

- **Affective** – feelings or emotions (general term that covers a broad range of feelings that people experience)
    - The six universal emotions are anger, fear, sadness, happiness, disgust and surprise
- **Cognitive** – beliefs or ideas
- **Behavioral** – how one intends to act

The three most prominent attitudes in organizational behavior are:

- **Job satisfaction** – positive feeling
- **Job involvement** – psychological identification
- **Organizational commitment** – maintain membership

Cognitive dissonance

Leon Festinger, an American psychologist, is responsible for the idea of cognitive dissonance**. Cognitive dissonance** (psychological discomfort) occurs when strongly held attitudes disagree with reality. People reduce cognitive dissonance in three main ways:

- Changing attitude and/or behavior
- Belittle the importance of the inconsistent behavior
- Rationalize away the dissonance

Values

A **value** is a core stable and enduring belief that guides behavior in all situations while an attitude is more specific. Rokeach identified two sets of values with 18 individual value items:

- **Terminal value** – desirable end-state

- **Instrumental** – behavior to achieve terminal value

People in same occupations, categories and/or age cohorts tend to hold similar values. Current value cohorts in the workplace are:

- **Veterans** – entered workforce in mid-1950s to early-1960s, loyal to employers
- **Baby Boomers** – entered workforce in mid-1960s through mid-1980s, more self-centered and focus is on self-success
- **Generation Xers**
- **Nexters** – expect relational opportunities and greater freedom in work

Learning Processes

Learning is a relatively permanent change based on experience. **Intelligence** is the capacity for constructive thinking, reasoning and problem solving. Howard Gardner's *Frames of Mind: The Theory of Multiple Intelligences* identifies seven intelligences:

- **Linguistic** – potential to learn new languages
- **Logical mathematical** – deductive reasoning and analysis
- **Musical** – appreciation, composition and performance
- **Spatial** – recognize and use patterns
- **Bodily** (kinesthetic) – mind and body for movement
- **Interpersonal** – understand and work with others
- **Intrapersonal** – understand and work with self
- **Naturalist** – live in harmony with the environment

Basic Models of Learning

The basic models of learning are:

- **Classical conditioning** – Ivan Pavlov experimented with an unconditioned stimulus (food) with conditioned stimulus (bell) to make a dog salivate (unconditioned response), when the dog heard the bell it would salivate (conditioned response)
- **Operant conditioning** – B.F. Skinner argued reinforcement strengthens behaviors making them more likely to be repeated, rewards are most effective if they immediately follow a desired response
- **Social learning** – assumes we learn from observation and experience, recognizes learning perceptions and how people respond to their perceptions of consequences

Learning organization

Many companies are becoming **learning organizations**. The characteristics of a learning organization are:

- Participatory in problem solving
- Celebrates risks taken in the interest of the organization
- Values team building and collaboration
- Empowers employee's creativity
- Open information flow

Training programs and methods

Training generally applies to learning short-term skills. Organizations tailor training to meet individual needs based on the present stage of a worker's career and their career path. Employees perform training "on-the-job" or "off-the-job," depending on the specific developmental needs of the company and individuals in the organization. The three training goals are:

- Increase job knowledge
- Improve organizational understanding
- Improve interpersonal skills

"**On the job**" methods of development include orientation, apprenticeship, job rotation, coaching, departmental meetings and company courses. "**Off the job**" methods of development include off-site seminars and tuition assistance.

Reinforcement theory

Psychologist Edward Thorndike's **law of effect** states behavior repeats when rewarded and disappears when it has an unfavorable result. B. F. Skinner concentrated on observable behavior (**behaviorism**). Skinner identified two distinct types of behaviors:

- **Respondent** – unlearned reflexes and stimulus responses
- **Operant** – learned behavior shaped by consequences

Skinner's theory to control behavior has four methods:

- **Positive reinforcement** – reward for desired behavior
- **Negative reinforcement** – removal of something unpleasant with a desired behavior
- **Punishment** – withdrawing a positive outcome or presenting a negative outcome to curb undesired behavior (e.g., docking employee's pay for tardiness)
- **Extinction** – ignoring/not reinforcing undesirable behavior

Reinforcement schedules have varying effectiveness:

- **Continuous reinforcement** – all desired behavior reinforced (appropriate for new or unstable behavior)
    - Behavior rapidly weakens if reinforcement is withheld and high frequency may lead to satiation
- **Intermittent reinforcement** – some of the desired behavior is reinforced, four types:
    - **Fixed-interval** – specific time intervals (e.g., pay checks); average and irregular performance
    - **Fixed-ratio** – specific number of desired behaviors (e.g., piece-rate pay); high and stable performance
    - **Variable-interval** – random times not picked by employee; moderately high and stable performance
    - **Variable-ratio** – random number of behaviors (e.g., slot machines); very high performance

Shaping is reinforcing closer and closer approximations of a desired behavior (also know as OB Mod). Managers can shape employee behavior by providing feedback, reinforcing quickly and continuously, using meaningful reinforcement and maintaining new behaviors with a variable schedule of reinforcement.

MOTIVATION

Motivation is a psychological process responsible for intensity, direction and persistence toward goal attainment. Motivating people to achieve organizational goals influences productivity. Motivation comes from two places:

- **Intrinsic reward** – positive feeling someone has while performing the action, there are four rewards;
    - Sense of meaningfulness
    - Sense of choice
    - Sense of competence
    - Sense of progress
- **Extrinsic rewards** – reward given to someone after the completion of an action

Job satisfaction is derived from fulfilling basic needs, meeting expectations, allowing fulfillment of values, feeling of being treated fairly (**equity**) and a general disposition of satisfaction. Unmotivated and dissatisfied employees increase turnover and stress. Motivational approaches fall into one of three areas:

- Traditional – economic rewards
- Human relations – treatment of employees, handling the employee as a whole person
- Contemporary theories

When dissatisfied, employees exhibit a variety of behaviors that are constructive or destructive and active or passive:

- **Exit** – looking for a new position
- **Voice** – actively trying to improve conditions
- **Loyalty** – passively waiting for things to improve
- **Neglect** – passively allowing conditions to worsen with reduced effort, more absenteeism and apathy

MOTIVATION THROUGH NEEDS

The needs theories identify internal motivational factors. The two most widely known need theories are:

- **McClelland's Need Theory** – three needs that motivate in varying degrees (achievement, affiliation, power), the most successful managers have a high power need and a low affiliation need
- **Maslow's Hierarchy of Needs** – five basic needs (see Figure 2) arranged by hierarchy, they must be achieved one at a time in ascending order (higher-order needs are the top three tiers)

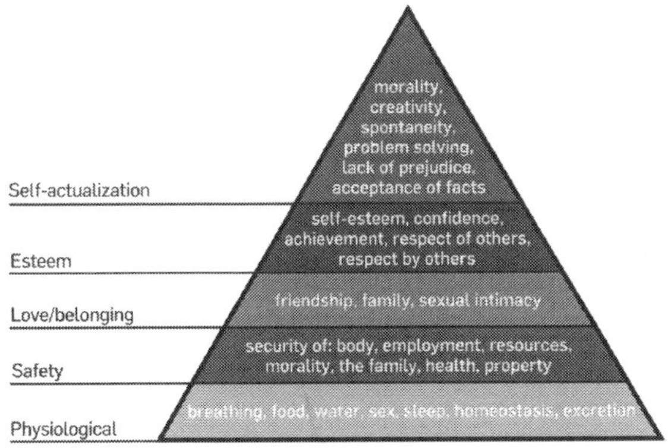

Figure 2: Maslow's Hierarchy of Needs
© Factoryjoe

Maslow referred to those few individuals that reach self-actualization as **Transcenders** and **Theory Z** people. He also opined that they are the happiest, most well adjusted people of all.

Alderfer built upon Maslow's hierarchy of needs categorizing needs into three main types (**ERG theory**):

- **Existence** – physiological and security factors
- **Relatedness** – being accepted by people
- **Growth** – self-esteem and self-actualization

Alderfer did not believe needs had to be satisfied in order. He also suggested the frustration over not being able to satisfy a higher-order need may lead to regression to lower need levels.

MOTIVATION THROUGH JOB DESIGN

Job design is altering specific jobs to increase satisfaction or performance. The four main approaches to job design are mechanistic, motivational, biological and perceptual-motor:

- **Mechanistic** – focus on most efficient means
    - Highly repetitive and simplified jobs, but workers dissatisfied, stressed and low sense of achievement
- **Motivational** – improve the intrinsic motivational factors
    - **Job rotation** – different jobs for variety
    - **Job enlargement** – variety through complexity
    - **Job enrichment** – inspired by Herzberg's motivational theory of **hygiene factors** (characteristics associated with dissatisfaction when not present, but do not motivate when present) and **motivators** (characteristics associated with satisfaction) modifies jobs by giving employees more ways to achieve, stimulate work, responsibility and advancement
    - **Job characteristics model** developed by Hackman and Oldham focuses on three areas:
        - **Core job dimensions** – skill variety, task identity, task significance, autonomy and feedback
        - **Critical psychological states** – the three factors correlate to core job dimensions
            - **Meaningfulness** – intrinsic rewards correlated to core dimensions of skill variety, task identity and task significance

        - **Responsibility for outcome** – correlated to the core job dimension of autonomy
        - **Knowledge of results** – related to the core job dimension of feedback
    - **Employee growth need**
- **Biological** – physiology, ergonomics and focuses on designing environment to minimize physical strain to reduce complaints
- **Perceptual-motor** – reliability of work outcomes with error rates, accident rates, feedback and equipment

Motivation through Equity

The **Equity Theory** (J. Stacy Adams) is the belief that motivation is through perceived fairness in social exchanges. Perceived inconsistences create cognitive dissonance that motivate remedial action. Equity in the workplace is based on inputs (e.g., training skills, seniority, efforts) and outputs (e.g., salary, promotions, recognition, benefits). The perception that someone is receiving greater outputs for similar inputs is **negative inequity**. The perception that someone is receiving lesser outcomes for similar inputs is **positive inequity**. Individuals have different thresholds for perceived inequities (**equity sensitivity**). The three thresholds of equity sensitivity are:

- **Benevolents** – high tolerance for negative inequity
- **Sensitives** – low tolerance for any inequity
- **Entitleds** – no tolerance for negative inequity, expectation is positive inequity

To correct inequity individuals will do one of three things:

- **Change inputs** (e.g., putting in less work)
- **Change outcomes** (e.g., asking for a raise or promotion)
- **Distort perceptions** (e.g., conclude that someone is working harder or has more experience)

Organizational justice is an expansion of the equity theory that focuses on the extent that people believe they are being treated fairly. There are three different components:

- **Distributive** – fairness of resource and reward distribution
- **Procedural** – fairness of allocation decisions, enhanced when employees feel they have a part in the decision
- **Interactional** – fairness of procedures implementation

Equity theory has several OB practical applications:

- Pay attention to employees' perceptions of fairness
- Allow employees to participate in decisions
- Implement organizational change fairly
- Monitor equity through conversations and surveys

MOTIVATION THROUGH EXPECTANCY

The **Expectancy Theory** (Vroom) bases motivation on a desired outcome. **Expectancy** is the belief that a degree of effort will lead to a level of performance (e.g., high effort more mastery). An individual's self esteem, self-efficacy, previous success and access to necessary materials affect expectancy. **Instrumentality** (belief that the outcome is contingent on level of performance) and **valence** (value individual has on outcome) affects motivation. Managers can increase motivation by:

- Rewarding for performance
- Designing challenging jobs
- Rewarding group accomplishments and cohesion
- Accommodating individuality and watching for inequities

MOTIVATION THROUGH GOAL-SETTING

The **Goal-Setting Theory** (Locke) bases motivation on accomplishing set goals. The management system is a management by objectives (MBO) model. **Management by objectives** systems incorporates participation in the decision process, goal-setting process and feedback. The four motivational mechanisms that goal-setting helps with are:

- Directs attention
- Regulates effort
- Increases persistence
- Encourages planning

Goals should follow the SMART acronym:

- **Specific** – precise (no ambiguity)
- **Measurable** – measurement device to assess
- **Attainable** – difficult but not unrealistic
- **Results oriented** – support organizational vision
- **Time bound** – have an end date

Managers can increase goal commitment by:

- Providing valuable outcomes

- Raising employees self-efficacy through training, role modeling and communicating confidence
- Employees make public commitment to goal
- Communicate the importance of the goal
- Allow employees role in setting goals
- Support rather than punish employees
- Breaking longer goals into shorter steps
- Ensure that employees have what is needed to reach goals

FEEDBACK

Feedback is objective information about performance. The two main functions of feedback are to instruct and motivate. Individuals have different desires and needs for feedback. When feedback is received, an individual perceives:

- Accuracy
- Credibility of the source
- Equity of the system
- Reasonableness of standards

Feedback from the entire system (peers, customers, managers) is **360-degree feedback**. Its advantages are:

- Useful in team-oriented environments
- More valid than a single-source
- Participative

Upward feedback (evaluation of superiors) is not often liked by managers and can be a personality contest. However, it can be a useful tool for development and training.

WORK STRESS AND THE INDIVIDUAL

There are two types of stress:

- **Eustress** – positive pressure toward accomplishment
- **Distress** – harmful stress accompanied by insecurity
    - The most severe stage of distress is **burnout** causing loss of productivity, frustration, and depression

Part III Interpersonal and group processes and characteristics

This test is divided among many areas of organizational behavior. This portion of the test will account for approximately 32 percent of the test questions. Part III will cover:

- Group dynamics
- Group behavior and conflict
- Leadership
- Power and politics
- Communication processes

Group dynamics

A **group** is two or more individuals that interact for shared goals with a common identity. There are two types of groups:

- **Formal** – created by the organization with three subtypes:
    - **Command** – relatively permanent work groups
    - **Task** – established by organization to solve a problem or accomplish a task (temporary)
    - **Affinity** – same level doing similar jobs join for information sharing and organizational issues
- **Informal** – formed via friendship or interest

Formal groups serve both the organization and the individual:

- Organizational
    - Achieve more complex tasks than individual can
    - Generates creative ideas and solutions
    - Coordinates among departments
    - Provides complex decisions and problem-solving
- Individual
    - Satisfies affiliation, self-esteem and identity
    - Opportunity to share perceptions of social reality
    - Reduces powerlessness feelings
    - Provides problem-solving for dilemmas

Teams

Teams are groups with skills that complement one another that hold themselves accountable to reach shared goals. They are becoming more popular because they routinely outperform individuals. A **team** is two or more people that generate a positive

synergy (the sum is greater than its parts). Not all groups are teams. There are several methods to make teams from groups:

- Investing in relationships (team-building activities)
- Modeling collaboration, mentoring and coaching
- Ensuring team members have the required skill set
- Assigning leaders that are task and relationship oriented
- Not too many strangers in a group

A relatively new kind of (and often times effective) team is the self-managed team. **Self-managed** teams have administrative oversight over their work. The team acts as its own supervisor and usually has expertise in different (but complementary) areas (**cross-functional**). Research suggests that self-managed teams have a positive effect on attitudes, productivity and do not affect turnover. Effective teams have four general categories:

- **Contextual** – adequate resources, effective leadership, trust and performance evaluation that reflect contributions
- **Composition** – abilities of members, personality, allocation of roles, diversity, size and member preferences
    - Most effective with ten or less members who are cross-trained and enjoy being group members
- **Work design** – freedom and autonomy to use skills
- **Process** – commitment to purpose, establishment of team goals, team efficacy, mental models, minimal social loafing and well-managed conflict

STAGES OF GROUP DEVELOPMENT

There are five stages of group development:

- **Stage I**: **Forming** – ice-breaking stage members are unclear and anxious about leadership and roles, if a formal leaders does not assert authority an emergent leader will
- **Stage II**: **Storming** – test policies and assumptions and figure out roles, power politics sometimes turn to rebellion
- **Stage III**: **Norming** – power questions resolved and team spirit sets in, the group becomes cohesive ("we" feeling)
- **Stage IV**: **Performing** –focus is reaching group goals
- **Stage V**: **Adjourning** – for temporary teams, the group disbands and returns to independence, sometimes marked by a celebration or feelings of loss

The **punctuated-equilibrium model** suggests that group activity is marked with long periods of inertia and acceleration of revolutionary change and activity as the deadline approaches.

Member roles

Member roles are either task oriented or maintenance oriented:

- Task roles
    - **Initiator** – suggests new ideas
    - **Information gatherer** – clarifies issues
    - **Opinion giver** – clarifies values
    - **Elaborator** – promotes understanding of issues
    - **Coordinator** – gathers ideas
    - **Orienter** – keeps group goal-oriented
    - **Evaluator** – tests groups effectiveness through measurement
    - **Energizer** – encourages group to accomplish more
    - **Procedural technician** – performs routine duties
    - **Recorder** – group memory function
- Maintenance roles
    - **Encourager** – fosters group solidarity and praises different point of views
    - **Harmonizer** – mediates conflicts
    - **Compromiser** – tries to bring together conflicting view points in a shared solution
    - **Gatekeeper** – encourages members to participate
    - **Standard setter** – evaluates processes
    - **Commentator** – records and documents dynamics
    - **Follower** – passive audience

Group behavior and conflict

Group **norms** are the shared attitudes, opinions, feelings or actions that guide the group's behavior. People that do not conform to group norms are rejected (**ostracized**). Norms of a group are developed in several methods:

- Statements by peers or supervisors
- Critical events in the history of an organization
- Primacy (first behavior patterns)
- Carryover from past situations

Groups can fall victim to specific dynamics that can affect productiveness:

- **Groupthink** – focus is on cohesiveness of the members and mental efficiency, reality and morals can deteriorate
    - Symptoms of groupthink are invulnerability, ignoring ethics, rationalizing, stereotyping opposition, not allowing debate, silence as consent, peer pressure and ignoring adverse information
    - Tactics to prevent groupthink are; critical evaluation, executive questioning, different groups explore same issues, subgroup debates, assigning a devil's advocate and rethinking decisions
- **Groupshift** – is a shift in viewpoint toward more risk
- **Social loafing** – the larger the group, the lesser the individual's effort; occurs most when output is not identifiable, members expected others would loaf and the task is perceived as unimportant or simple

LEVELS OF CONFLICT

There are three main theories of conflict:

- **Traditional view** – all conflict is unhealthy
- **Human relations view** – conflict is natural in groups and should be managed but not eliminated
- **Interactionist view** – conflict can be functional or dysfunctional, it can also be classified by type:
    - **Task** – contents and goals of work (low to moderate levels are functional)
    - **Relationship** – interpersonal conflict (nearly always dysfunctional)
    - **Process** – how work gets done (low levels are functional)

STAGES OF CONFLICT

There are five stages of conflict:

- **Potential opposition** – opportunities for a conflict
    - Communication (e.g., semantics, misunderstanding, "noise" in communication)
    - Structure (e.g., specialization, leadership style, reward system, dependence)
    - Personal (e.g., personality, emotions, values)
- **Cognition** and **personalization** – parties have to perceive a conflict and become emotionally involved

- **Intentions** – individuals develop styles for dealing with conflict; there are five primary styles of conflict handling:
    - **Dominating (forcing, competing)** – assertiveness to get one's way; used for emergencies and urgent developments, but likely resented
    - **Avoiding** – tackling issue more trouble than worth
    - **Compromising** – both parties have power and say
    - **Obliging (smoothing, accommodating)** – neglects self-needs more concerned with peace; encourages cooperation but is a temporary fix
    - **Integrating (problem solving, collaborating)** – parties outline problem and weigh alternatives; good for misunderstandings not opposing values
- **Behavior** – conflict becomes visible with statements, actions and reactions
- **Outcomes** – **functional conflict** serves an organization's interests, and **dysfunctional conflict** threatens an organization's interests. Functional conflict has three desired outcomes:
    - Agreement
    - Stronger relationships
    - Learning

To promote functional conflict manager's can:

- **Devil's advocacy** – assign someone the role of critic to question assumptions
- **Dialectic method** – create a debate with opposing views to understand an issue

CONFLICT MANAGEMENT

To deal with conflict it is important to understand there are several sources of conflict, including:

- Competition for scarce resources
- Role ambiguity
- Communication
- Personality incompatibility
- Power
- Conflicting goals

Managers can address organizational conflict by:

- Focusing on superordinate goals and need for cooperation

- Bargaining with group members capable of logically focusing and setting aside personality differences, two main types of bargaining are:
    - **Distributive** – single issue where one person gains at expense of another (involves win/lose strategies)
    - **Integrative** – multiple issues, seeks a win/win solution, the **added-value negotiation** is an integrative tactic which involves; clarifying interests, identifying options, designing packages, agreeing on a deal and perfecting the deal
- Mediation through an uninterested party
- Communicate by focusing on facts, investigating alternatives, balancing power and not forcing consensus

Alternative resolution procedure (ARD)

Alternative resolution procedures (ARD) are different methods of employee resolution procedures to resolve conflict:

- **Step-review system** – sequentially higher management
- **Facilitation** – third-party encourages conflicting parties to deal directly
- **Conciliation** – neutral third-party is communication conduit; appropriate for parties that will not meet
- **Peer-review** – group of employee and management representatives that act as a jury and render a decision
- **Open-door policy** – settling disputes with various levels of management above the supervisor
- **Ombudsman** – designated individual whom employees can seek counsel and resolution
- **Mediation** – neutral party hears both sides, does not rend decision up to the disputants to reach a mutual decision
- **Arbitration** –neutral party renders a decision

Leadership

Not all managers are leaders; **leadership** is the ability to influence people. The three broad types of skills leaders have are:

- Technical – knowledge and ability
- Human – work with people
- Conceptual – think in terms of models, frameworks and broad relationships

Models of leadership

The three basic models of leadership are:

- **Authoritarian** – dictatorship dismissing team input
- **Democratic** – open lines of communication between workers and management; values team input and cooperation without being overly active in teams
- **Laissez-faire** – hands off approach over all decision-making without further involvement unless asked

Types of leaders

There are many types of leaders and different styles work for different situations. The types of leaders include:

- **Transactional leader** – clarifies roles, initiates structure, provides rewards, and is considerate of employees; fair, hard-working and tolerant with focus on job needs
- **Charismatic leader** – visionaries motivate employees to go beyond expectations; emphasize inspiration, vision and modeling, capable and team-oriented
- **Transformational leader** – ability to bring innovation by recognizing employee needs; creative solutions, pay attention to concerns and developmental needs of followers, encourage creativity, ambitious goals and are able to excite and inspire followers
- **Servant leader** – prioritization on fulfilling employees' needs and goals balanced with the mission; needs of organization, customer and community above self
- **Authentic leaders** – know who they are and what they believe in, they act on those beliefs openly and candidly

Leadership in theory

There is no one right approach to leadership; however, most agree that managers can learn to become leaders:

- **Trait theories** – emphasize leadership characteristics
    - **Leadership prototype** – (Lord, 1986) depiction of traits that a person believes identifies leadership
- **Behavioral theories** – task-oriented and relationship oriented behavioral differences between effective and ineffective leaders; stresses leadership can be learned and there is no one best style

    - **Ohio State Studies** – concluded two independent dimensions of leadership; consideration (creating mutual respect and trust) and initiation (identification of what members should do)
    - **University of Michigan Studies** – similar to the Ohio State Studies except the two styles are; employee centered and job centered
    - The **managerial grid** conceptualizes the framework presented by Ohio State and Michigan; grid maps dimensions based on "concern for people" and "concern for production", managers high on both ends perform the best
- **Situational theories** – stress situational variables, rather than characteristics of the individual manager; links leadership with readiness of the organization. The three dimensions of situational control are leader/member relations (e.g., trust and loyalty), task structure and position power. The main situational theories are:
    - **Fiedler's Contingency Model** – matches leader style with the situation that is conducive
        - Stress is key in determining effectiveness, intelligence is more effective in a stress-free environment, and experience more effective high-stress conditions
        - Leader's style is determined by their score on the **least preferred co-workers** (LPC) questionnaire that measures the degree that the respondent enjoys working with the person they dislike the most
        - Leadership style is fixed; if one is not conducive to the other, either the leader or the situation must change
    - **Path-Goal Theory** – (House, 1970 revised 1996) leader's behave to compliment staff's abilities and compensate for deficiencies; they guide workers to choose best paths to reach personal and organizational goals and different leadership behaviors are needed depending on situation:

        - **Participative** – leaders consult followers and ask for input before decision; for followers personally involved with work
        - **Directive** – leader advises followers what is expected and tells them how to perform the task; when role and tasks are ambiguous and intrinsically satisfying
        - **Achievement-oriented** – leader sets challenging goals and expects followers to perform (e.g. scientists, salespeople)
        - **Supportive** – leaders shows concern for well-being of followers; high stress
    - **Hersey and Blanchard Situational Leadership Theory** – based on the follower's ability (maturity levels) and willingness to complete tasks
        - **Telling** – one-way communication from manager to subordinate
        - **Selling** – two-way communication; provide support and allow subordinate to influence
        - **Participating** – sharing decision-making
        - **Delegating** – leader passes some powers to group or individual and monitors
    - **Leader member exchange theory** – behave more favorable toward follower when they are a member of the leader "in group"
    - **Leader-participation model** – (Vroom, Yetton) leader behavior adjusts to reflect task structure in a seven-step decision tree (five leadership styles)

POWER AND POLITICS

Organizational politics is the intentional enhancement of self-interest. Uncertainty prompts political behavior. **Social influence** is the measurement of our interpersonal interaction and success of influencing others. There are nine generic influence tactics:

- **Rational persuasion** – use of logic and facts, the only power tactic that is effective across organizational levels
- **Inspirational appeals** – generating enthusiasm
- **Consultation** – getting others to participate
- **Ingratiation** – putting someone in a good mood
- **Personal appeals** – using friendship and loyalties

- **Exchange** – trading favors
- **Coalition** – getting others to help in persuasion
- **Pressure** – demanding compliance
- **Legitimating** – requests based on authority or right

Attempting to influence someone will result in commitment (substantial agreement), compliance (reluctant agreement) or resistance. Organizations can keep politics within reasonable limits by screening out overly political people in hiring, open-book management, ensure understanding of organization at all levels, establish formal conflict resolution and publicly recognizing and rewarding members.

Types of power

A significant difference between a manager and a leader is the source of their power. Three types of power come from the position in an organization:

- **Legitimate** – position in company
- **Reward** – power of rewards
- **Coercive** – power of punishment

Two types of power come from personal sources (and are the most effective of all powers):

- **Expert** – level of expertise
- **Referent** – degree which individual is admired

Leader roles

Leaders play multiple roles depending on the situation. Though some prefer one style of management to another, the successful leader is able to adopt many roles. Henry Mintzberg grouped leader roles into three main types with ten sub roles:

- **Decisional** – strategic planning and using resources
    - **Entrepreneur** – expand businesses (top-level)
    - **Disturbance handler** – dealing with internal and external issues (any management level)
    - **Resource allocator** – distributing organizational resources to appropriate departments and projects
    - **Negotiator** – reaching agreements with others regarding products, services, pay and benefits
- **Interpersonal** – direction and supervision
    - **Figurehead** – communicates goals and ethical expectations, performs symbolic ceremonial duties

- **Leader** – visionary that energizes and empowers employees, decision-maker
    - **Liaison** – links people and projects through shared resources, maintains self-developed network for information and favors
- **Informational** – obtaining and transferring information
    - **Monitor** – monitors information in the environment
    - **Disseminator** – communicates changes/visions
    - **Spokesperson** – makes major announcements and deals with press and advertising

LEVELS OF ORGANIZATIONAL POLITICS

There are three levels of organizational politics.

- **Individual** – self-interests are pursued by the individual
- **Coalition** – temporary groups pursuing a single issue
- **Network** – loose associations of individuals seeking social support for general self-interests

POLITICAL TACTICS

The most frequent political tactics in an organization include; networking with the right contacts, using key players, bending rules, self-promotion, blaming others and impression management. The most likely people that will engage in political behaviors are:

- High self-monitors
- Internal locus of control
- High need for power

Politics happen most when organizational resources are scarce, trust is low, roles ambiguous, and performance evaluations are unclear, high pressure to perform and self-serving management.

COMMUNICATION PROCESSES

Communication is the transfer of information between people. There are eight-steps to communication:

1. **Develop an idea** – sender thinks of what they want to say
2. **Encode** – converts the idea into words or writing
3. **Transmit** – delivers idea to recipient
4. **Receive** – another person receives message
5. **Decode** – receiver tries to understand meaning
6. **Accept** – receiver accepts or rejects message

7. **Use** – receiver uses information or stores it
8. **Provide feedback** – receiver acknowledges receipt

It is important to choose an appropriate communication channel to ensure effective communication. A rich channel is needed for communication that is personal (e.g., performance feedback). The characteristics of a rich channel are:

- Handles multiple cues simultaneously
- Allows for rapid feedback
- Very personal

Some common problems with effective communication are:

- **Polarization** – strong disagreement on an issue
- **Defensive reasoning** – abandonment of logic to try to avoid embarrassment of a losing stance in an argument
- **Cognitive dissonance** – against receiver's values
- **Face-saving** – trying to preserve self-concept from attack

Symbols used to communicate include:

- **Words** – the context which something is said
    - **Social cues** – the cues from the social environment
    - **Readability** –understandability of the written word, can be improved by simple words, short sentences with clear structure and action verbs
- **Pictures** – used to clarify words (e.g., charts, maps)
- **Nonverbal communication** – action (or failure to act)
    - **Credibility gap** – difference between what someone says and their actions
    - **Body language** – includes stance, facial expression, physical touch, sighing and yawning

COMMUNICATION BARRIERS

There are several ways that communication barriers can limit a receiver's understanding and act as **noise**. The three types of communication barriers are:

- **Personal barriers** – originate from human emotion, values, stereotypes, big egos, listening skills, education, race, sex, socioeconomic status and others
    - **Psychological distance** – emotional separation from the sender, causing someone to "tune out"
- **Physical barriers** – interferences from the environment
    - **Ecological controls** – physical barriers that can be altered (e.g., desk openness)

- **Proxemics** – the study of how much spatial separation is culturally acceptable

- **Semantic barriers** – the science of meaning and limitations of the symbols used to communicate (prevalent when cultures mingle)
    - **Inference** – the interpretation of a symbol based on previous assumptions
    - **Jargon** – specialized language to a profession

Communication styles

There are three basic types of communication styles:

- **Assertive** – pushes hard to communicate without attacking and allows others to impact; expressive without intruding
    - Good eye contact, firm and comfortable posture, appropriate facial expressions with selective disruptions that allow for understanding
    - Uses direct language (e.g., "I" and "we")
- **Aggressive** – seeks to take unfair advantage of others
    - Glaring eyes, too close, threatening gestures (e.g., pointing fingers), speaks loudly and interrupts
    - Uses swear words or abusive language, evaluates others and threatens
- **Nonassertive** – allows others to take advantage of them
    - Little eye contact, weak voices and looks down
    - Uses language fillers (e.g., "um"), qualifiers (e.g., "kind of") and negates (e.g., "I'm not sure")

Communication networks

The communication networks in an organization are:

- **Downward communication** – from management to subordinates (instruction, performance feedback, news)
    - Quality over quantity is best; employees can suffer from **communication overload** (receipt of more communication than understandable at one time)
- **Upward communication** – from subordinates to management; best practices include questioning (open and closed), active listening, and meetings, there are many difficulties with upward communication:
    - **Delay** – slow movement of information
    - **Filtering** – screening of information
    - **Short-circuiting** – skipping management levels

    - **Need for response** – deters further communication
    - **Distortion** – changing reality for self-objectives
- **Lateral communication (cross-communication)** – across chains of command, usually the most dominant kind
    - **Boundary spanners** – strong communication skills within and outside their department
    - **Network** – group of people who exchange information about shared interests
    - **Ombudsperson** – person that responds to complaints, policy clarifications or allegations

Organizational communication has four major types:

- **Formal small-group networks** – **chain** (follows chain of command), **wheel** (central figure acts as a conduit) and **all-channel** (all groups actively communicate)
- **Informal communication** – the grapevine is a fast and influential information tool that can lack accuracy (used by 75 percent of employees), it is highest with insecurities
    - To prevent **negative rumors**, management can refute, not repeat and remove the reason for it
- **Electronic communication** – emails, texts, etc.
- **Knowledge management** – distributing collective wisdom of organization

ACTIVE LISTENING

There are nine tips to active listening:

1. Do not talk
2. Make talker feel comfortable
3. Show talker you are willing to listen (e.g., eye contact)
4. Remove distractions
5. Empathize and connect
6. Be patient (no interrupting)
7. Pause before responding (hold temper)
8. Try not to criticize or argue
9. Ask questions to understand

There are five listening styles:

- **Appreciative** – listens to appreciate (e.g., music)
- **Empathetic** – focuses on emotions
- **Comprehensive** – focuses on understanding
- **Discerning** – focuses on main points
- **Evaluative** – listens to challenge or formulate arguments

Part IV Organizational processes and characteristics

This test is divided among many areas of organizational behavior. This portion of the test will account for approximately 19 percent of the test questions. Part IV will cover:

- Organizational decision-making
- Organizational structure
- Organization design

The **organizational environment** are all factors that the organization has no power to control. Organizations must be aware of both the external and internal environments:

- External (**macroenvironment**) – factors that can affect organizational strategies
  - **Sociological** – customs, lifestyles and values of the society in which the business operates
  - **Technological** – advancements impacting the company and society
  - **Political-legal** – laws (federal, state, local) and pressure groups influencing social responsibility
  - **Economic** – monetary health of the country/region where organization operates
  - **Global** – significant events in foreign countries
  - **Task environment** – customers, competitors, suppliers and labor markets
- Internal (**microenvironment**) – internal resources
  - **Financial** – availability of funds for growth
  - **Physical factors** – raw materials, equipment and distributing facilities
  - **Human factors** – people resources (employees)
  - **Technological** – company's needs and the applied technology currently employed

Organizational decision-making

The two main groups of decision-making models are rational and nonrational. The rational model's strengths are high-quality decisions, transparent reasoning and discouraging bias in decisions. The **rational model** is a six-step process that assumes complete information, lack of bias and maximum payoff:

- Identification of the problem

- Identifying decision criteria
- Weighing previously identified criteria
- Generating a set of solutions
- Rating each solution based on criteria
- Computing optimal solution

The nonrational model attempts to describe how decisions are actually made versus the rational (how they should be made). The two main nonrational models developed by Herbert Simon are:

- Simon's **normative model** – constraints restrict us from rational decision-making (**bounded rationality**), actually **satisficing** (or choosing a "good enough" alternative)
- **Garbage can model** – decision-making is sloppy and based on interaction of problems, solutions and participants

Types of Ethical Decisions

Ethical decisions have two sides, the individual versus the organization. There are five main approaches to ethical decisions:

- **Utilitarian** – (Mill) the greatest good for the greatest number is ethical, most commonly used in business; values efficiency, productivity and profits
- **Individualism** – morality is based on the long-term interests of an individual; values honesty and integrity
- **Integrative social contracts theory** – existing norms
- **Moral** – fundamental rights; values consent, privacy, conscience, free speech, due process, life and safety
- **Justice** – decisions should be impartial

When an organization focuses on means as well as outcomes with a high-risk tolerance, it encourages ethical decisions.

Decision-Making Biases

There are eight decision-making biases that affect abilities:

- **Availability heuristic** – readily available information in memory (most recent or evoking strong emotions)
- **Representativeness heuristic** – likelihood of something occurring based on impressions of similar events
- **Confirmation bias** – subconscious decision before investigation; seeks only information supporting decision
- **Anchoring bias** – influenced by first information received about a decision (even if not relevant)

- **Overconfidence bias** – overly optimistic about abilities
- **Hindsight bias** – the actual outcome influences the belief that it could have been predicted
- **Framing bias** – influenced by how a question is asked
- **Escalation of commitment bias** – sticking with a bad decision and investing more time and effort in it

Knowledge management (sharing knowledge through the organization) is an effective weapon against poor decisions.

Individual decision making

A manager's style and personality largely influence decisions. There are four major decision styles:

- **Directive** – preference for simple solutions; made quickly with reliance on existing rules, has a low tolerance for ambiguity; task-oriented with a strong factual focus
- **Analytical** – data collection with careful consideration of alternatives; high tolerance for ambiguity
- **Conceptual** – reliance on a lot of information, engaging people in process; more socially oriented than analytical; high tolerance for ambiguity; long-term perspective approach with reliance on discussions and intuition
- **Behavioral** – preference on the individuals in the organization; concerned with personnel development

Intuition and creativity both play a role in an individual's decision-making process. **Intuition** is the capacity of knowledge or understanding without logic. **Holistic hunch intuition** is based on a subconscious integration of information stored in memory; while **automated experience intuition** is a decision based on familiarity of a situation. Gender also plays a role in decisions, as women tend to spend more time evaluating a decision than men. **Creativity** is the process of finding a new solution or innovation. There are five stages to creativity:

- **Preparation** – tacit and explicit knowledge
- **Concentration** – focusing on problem
- **Incubation** – unconsciously thinking of the problem
- **Illumination** – conscious generation of an idea
- **Verification** – trying the new idea

Group decision-making

Studies suggest that the more diverse a team the more innovative, significant and useful the decisions are. There are several advantages to group decision-making including; more knowledge, different perspectives, greater comprehension, increased acceptance and training. However, group decision-making also has several disadvantages:

- Social pressure to conform
- Domination of the vocal
- Logrolling (political dealing to displace better ideas)
- Goal displacement (e.g., concentrating on "winning")
- Groupthink

There are practices to avoid the disadvantages of group decisions:

- **Brainstorming** – idea generation tool with specific rules (defer judgment, build on ideas, stay focused, wild ideas, quantity over quality, visual, one conversation at a time); brainstorming is effective for generating new ideas, but not to select the solution
- **Nominal group technique** – process generates ideas and evaluates solutions
    - Group meets to discuss and understand the issue
    - Individuals silently generate ideas in writing
    - Round-robin recitation of each solution recording ideas publically (no discussion)
    - Once all ideas are posted, the group discusses them
    - Group members anonymously vote for solution
- **Delphi** – generates anonymous ideas and judgments from people that are dispersed; useful when in-person meetings are not reasonable, group has a tendency toward groupthink or when few people dominate
- **Computer-aided** – used to reduce roadblocks, two types:
    - **Chauffeur-driven** – asks predetermined questions and computer tabulates responses
    - **Group-driven** – special facilities where input is on a large projector and is anonymous

Organizational structure

Organizational structure is the division of tasks into resources. An official organization chart shows the positions of those who make up a company and illustrate the formal organizational structure, including responsibility, authority and accountability. Organizational structure includes:

- Formal tasks assigned to departments and individuals
- Identifies reporting relationships and chains of command
- Illustrates coordination of employees and departments

DIMENSIONS OF ORGANIZATIONAL STRUCTURE

There are four main dimensions of an organization:

- **Specialization** – degree that tasks are divided into jobs; too much specialization encourages boredom (e.g., assembly line) and too little causes inefficiencies
- **Chain of command** – the line of authority
    - **Unity of command** – each person is held accountable to a single manager
    - **Scalar principle** – line of authority includes all individuals and everyone knows who they report to
    - **Authority** – three characteristics; title, acceptance of the authority by subordinates and increasing authority in higher levels of the chain of command
- **Management span** – number of employees that report to a supervisor (**span of control**)
    - Management span is based on co-workers tasks, centralization of location, support systems, direction required, and personal preference
    - **Tall (vertical) structure** – narrow span of control; many levels
    - **Flat structure** – large span of control; few levels
- **Centralization** – decision-making level
    - Centralized organizations keep decision-making near the top; decentralized organizations grant lower levels of authority decision-making power
    - Centralization is affected by uncertainty (decentralizes decisions), organizational strategy and times of crises (centralizes decisions)

ORGANIZATION DESIGN

There are three main organizational designs:

- **Simple structure** – low degree of departmentalization, wide spans of control, authority centralized to a single person and little formalization (small businesses)

- Advantages: Fast, accountable, flexible and inexpensive
    - Disadvantages: slow decision-making, low formalization and high centralization
- **Bureaucracy** – routine operating tasks, formalized rules, tasks groups via functional departments, centralized authority, narrow spans of control
    - Advantages: efficient standardized activities
    - Disadvantages: functional unit goals sometimes override overall goals and programmed decisions can be ineffective
- **Matrix** – combines two forms of departmentalization (functional and product)
    - Advantages: better communication and flexibility
    - Disadvantages: violates unity of command with two chains of command, confusion and stress

There are two new designs that are used (though less often):

- **Virtual organization** – majority functions outsourced, highly centralized with little or no departmentalization
    - Advantage: flexibility
    - Disadvantage: management has less control
- **Boundaryless organization** – flattens organizations with cross-hierarchical teams, participative decisions and uses extranets and intranets to communicate
    - Advantages: flexibility, alliances, eliminates chain of command, limitless spans of control

Organizational structures can be classified in two ways:

- **Mechanistic** – extensive departmentalization, high formalization, limited information sharing, little participation by lower levels for decisions
- **Organic** – flat, cross-hierarchal and cross-functional teams, low formalizations, robust information sharing and high decision-making participation

Organizations select a mechanistic or organic structure based on:

- Strategy – innovation (organic), cost minimization (mechanistic) and imitation (combination)
- Size – as organizations increase in size they typically become more mechanistic (2,000+ employees almost always are mechanistic)

- Technology – degree of routineness is positively correlated with mechanistic structures
- Environment – stable environments prefer mechanistic structures, uncertain environments favor organic structures
    - Capacity – support of growth
    - Volatility – instability
    - Complexity – degree of uniqueness

Organizing structure for flat organizations

To become more flexible and responsive to the ever-changing landscape of business many organizations are opting for a flatter structure. Flatter organizational structures lead to better coordination between departments. To improve coordination, organizations use task forces, teams and project management:

- **Task forces** – short-term, cross-functional teams to resolve a specific problem
- **Teams** – representatives from different departments who meet to resolve routine issues and improve communication
- **Project management** – coordination of activities across several departments from inception to completion

Typically, flatter organizations share the following characteristics:

- Shared information through all levels of the organization (**open-book management**)
- Decentralized and participative decision-making
- More importance on organizational goals in the individual departments and values risks in the interest of goals
- **Egalitarian culture** – focus on community and caring

Part V Change and development processes

This test is divided among many areas of organizational behavior. This portion of the test will account for approximately seven percent of the test questions. Part V will cover:

- Basic processes and concepts of change
- Applications and techniques of change and development

Basic processes and concepts of change

Change has become a constant in today's organizations. Changes include technology, products and structural (management).

Pressures for change

Pressure for change can originate externally or internally:

- The four main external pressures for change are demographic (diversity), technology, customer and market changes and societal/political pressures.
- Internal pressures for change originate inside the organization, and include job satisfaction, productivity, turnover and conflict.

Models and processes for planned organizational change

Lewin's three-stage planned change model is:

1. **Unfreezing** – motivating new behaviors, **benchmarking** (comparing performance of organization to high-performing competitors) to motivate change
2. **Changing** – new processes, procedures or equipment
3. **Refreezing** – the new processes become stabilized

Kotter created an eight-step method to organizational change:

1. Establish urgency
2. Guide coalition (cross-functional with power)
3. Develop strategy
4. Communicate change vision
5. Empower action
6. Generate short-term wins
7. Consolidate gains and produce additional change
8. Anchor new approaches

The system change model assumes a bigger picture approach with four main components:

1. **Inputs** – analysis of internal strengths and weaknesses and external opportunities and threats (SWOT)

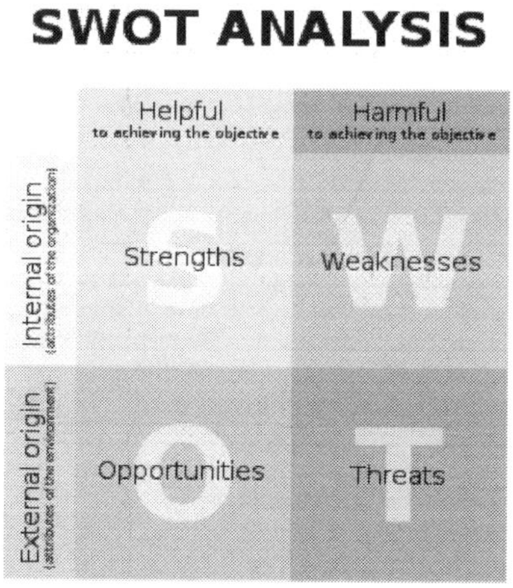

Figure 3: SWOT Analysis
© Xhienne

2. **Strategic plans** – strategies and goals that include a long term goal and actions needed to reach it
3. **Target elements of change** – organizational arrangements, people, methods and social factors
4. **Outputs** – organizational, department group and individual level (the desired inputs of the change)

RESISTANCE TO ORGANIZATIONAL CHANGE

People resist change for a variety of reasons, including:

- People are ingrained with a predisposition toward change
- Fear of the unknown
- Climate of mistrust
- Fear of failure
- Loss of status or job security
- Peer pressure
- Disruption of traditions and group relationships
- Personality conflicts
- Lack of tact or bad timing
- Nonreinforcing reward systems
- Complacency because of past success

Management can overcome resistance to change with six strategies depending on the organizational circumstance:

1. **Education/communication** – once persuaded people usually help facilitate; time consuming
2. **Participation/support** – initiators do not have all data and face powerful resistors, participants "buy-in" and will commit to change they helped produce; time consuming and management has to watch for unsuitable changes
3. **Facilitation/agreement** – best for adjustment problems; can be time consuming and still fail
4. **Negotiation/agreement** – when a powerful group will lose out in the change, can avoid resistance; expensive
5. **Manipulation/co-optation** – other tactics are too expensive or fail, quick and easy solution; can breed discontent about feeling manipulated
6. **Explicit/implicit coercion** –when speed is vital and change initiators have power; can leave people angry

ORGANIZATIONAL CULTURE CHANGE

Organizational change is tackled trough targeting the culture (observable artifacts, values or basic assumptions). An organization can change culture via several mechanisms:

- Statements regarding philosophy, values and mission
- Design of physical spaces
- Slogans, sayings, mottos and stories
- Role models, training, teaching, mentoring
- Rewards and status symbols
- Leaders reactions to crises
- Workflow and organizational structure
- Organizational systems and procedures
- Goals used for selection, layoffs and retirement

APPLICATIONS AND TECHNIQUES OF CHANGE AND DEVELOPMENT

Organizational development is not a systematic approach to change, it is a set of techniques used to implement planned change and for an organization to improve itself. The characteristics of organizational development are; profound and deep change, value loaded change, process-oriented focus and research with practical implications.

List of Appendices

Appendix	Description
A	Percentages of Test Topic Questions
B	Classic Management Perspective
C	Humanistic Management Perspective
D	Major Federal Employment Laws
E	Big Five Personality Traits
F	Emotional Intelligence
G	Dominant Culture Dimensions
H	GLOBE Project

Appendix A: Percentages of Test Questions

Percentage	Curriculum Content
6%	**Overview of the organizational behavior field:** • The field of organizational behavior • The study of organizational behavior
36%	**Individual processes and characteristics:** • Perceptual processes • Personality • Attitudes • Learning processes • Motivation • Work stress and the individual
32%	**Interpersonal and group processes and characteristics:** • Group dynamics • Group behavior and conflict • Leadership • Power and politics • Communication processes
19%	**Organizational processes and characteristics:** • Organizational decision-making • Organization structure • Organization design
7%	**Change and development processes:** • Basic processes and concepts of change • Applications and techniques of change and development

Appendix B: Classic Perspective

The classic management perspective emphasizes a rational and scientific approach to management. Below are the major subfields of this study and the characteristics of the approach.

Subfield	**Major characteristics**
Scientific Management	• To improve labor scientifically proven changes
Bureaucratic Organizations	• Select workers with abilities • Wage incentives for better labor • Right person for the right job • No focus on social context of job • No individual treatment • Ignore ideas and suggestions
Administrative Principles	• Focus on the total organization in lieu of the worker • Unity of command • Specialized work • Similar activities grouped together • Scalar chain

Appendix C: Humanistic Perspective

The humanistic management perspective focuses on human behavior, needs, and attitudes. Below are the major subfields of this study and the characteristics of the approach.

Subfield	**Major characteristics**
Human Relations Movement	• Emphasize satisfaction of basic needs and improves productivity • Hawthorne studies revealed employees worked better when they had better treatment
Human Resources Perspective	• Design job to meet higher-level needs (according to Abraham Maslow's hierarchy of needs) • Theory X and Theory Y
Behavioral Sciences Approach	• Apply social science to organizations

Appendix D: Major federal Employment laws

Year	Law	Effect
1963	Equal Pay Act	Same pay despite gender
1964	Civil Rights Act, Title VII	No discrimination based on gender, age, color, religion, national origin
1967	Age Discrimination in Employment	Restricts mandatory retirement and outlaws age discrimination
1970	Occupational Safety and Health Act (OSHA)	Mandatory safety standards in the workplace
1972	Equal Employment Opportunity Act	Coverage of the Civil Rights Act of 1964 broadened to state and local governments and public and private educational institutions
1978	Pregnancy Discrimination Act of 1978	Cannot discriminate against a woman because of pregnancy
1990	Americans with Disabilities Act	Prevents discrimination against employees who are physically or mentally handicap
1991	Civil Rights Act	No discrimination based on sex, religion, national origin, and disability; discriminated can seek damages
1993	Family Medical Leave Act (FMLA)	Employers provide up to 12 weeks of unpaid leave for birth, adoption or familial emergency
1994	Uniformed Services Employment and Reemployment Rights	Military deployment for a short service have home jobs secured during absence

Appendix E: Big Five Personality Traits

Trait	**Definition**
Extroversion	Degree of talkativeness, assertiveness and comfort with relationships
Agreeableness	Degree of cooperation, forgiveness, understanding and trust
Conscientiousness	Degree of responsibility, dependability and achievement orientation
Emotional stability	Degree of serenity, enthusiasm and security
Openness	Degree of interests, imagination, creativity and consideration of novel ideas

Appendix F: Emotional Intelligence

Trait	**Definition**
Self-awareness	Aware of self-feeling, knowing self-strengths and limits with a sound sense of self-worth
Self-management	Ability to keep impulses in check, honesty, flexibility, drive to improve performance, readiness and optimism
Social Awareness	Empathy, reading organizational currents, recognizing and meeting needs in others
Relationship Management	Ability to motivate, influence, develop others, change, build bonds and collaborate

Appendix G: Dominant culture dimensions

Hofstede identified five dominant dimensions across cultures.

Dimension	**Definition**
Power distance	The amount of accepted unequal distribution of power
Individualism vs. Collectivism	Focus on self vs. group goals
Masculinity vs. Feminity	Focus on work vs. focus on others
Uncertainty avoidance	Reliance on social norms and rules to avoid unpredictability
Long-term vs. short-term orientation	Focus on long-term goals or short term goals

U.S. citizens tend to be individualistic and short-term, scoring low on uncertainty avoidance and power distance. They score high on masculinity (e.g., traditional gender roles).

Appendix H: GLOBE Project

GLOBE confirms the validity of Hofstede's five dimensions and adds four more. The GLOBE (Global Leadership and Organizational Behavior Effectiveness) project theorizes predictions of behavior based on specific cultural variables. The nine dimensions are:

Dimension	**Definition**
Power distance	The amount of unequal distribution of power that is accepted
Uncertainty avoidance	Reliance on social norms and rules to avoid unpredictability
Institutional collectivism	How much leaders should encourage the collected group or individual goals
In-group collectivism	How much pride for their organization
Gender egalitarianism	Tolerance between genders in workplace
Assertiveness	Confrontation tolerance
Future orientation	Delay gratification by planning for future
Performance orientation	Reward for improvement or excellence
Humane orientation	Encouragement for kindness and generosity

Glossary

Because this is a study guide, some of these words are found throughout the text, however there are some new ones, be sure you understand the meanings to all of these words because they will help you exponentially during the multiple choice test.

360-degree feedback – process that uses multiple raters to appraise employees and guide in development

A

Ability – characteristic responsible for an individual's maximum physical or mental performance

Absenteeism – not reporting to work

Acceptance theory of authority – authority dependent on subordinate's acceptance of manager's right to lead

Accommodation – goals compatible and interaction between groups is unimportant for goal attainment

Accountability – responsibility for actions

Achievement motivation – drive to overcome challenges and achieve goals

Achievement tests – measures current abilities

Action research – process of identification of system problems, gathering data, correcting, assessing progress, making adjustments and learning

Activity based costing – control system that allocate costs for each activity that goes into a product or service

Active listening – listening to understand without judgment, receiving both the factual and emotional messages

Added-value negotiation – cooperatively developing multiple deal packages and building long term relationships

Administrative principles – focuses on total organization rather than the individual

Adhocracy culture – work culture with external focus and flexibility

Adjourning – ending stage of team development

Adult ego state – psychological position that results in demonstration of unemotional behavior

Adverse impact – rejection of higher percentage of a protected class for employment compared to non-protected class
Affective component – part of attitude that relates to feeling
Affiliation motivation – drive to relate to people socially
Affirmative action – policy that requires employers to guarantee equal employment for people in minority groups
Aggressive style – takes unfair advantage of others to get ahead
Agreeableness – person's ability to get along with others
Alarm reaction – response to stress characterized by elevated heart rate, increased respiration and adrenaline
Alienation – feeling of powerlessness, no meaning, lonely with no attachment to the job, work or organization
All-channel network – all people communicate with one another
Alternative dispute resolution – resolving disputes through mediation and arbitration
Analytical style – decision-making style that relies on a lot of information and careful evaluation of all alternatives
Analytics – process of making decisions based on evidence
Anticipatory socialization – information learned about careers, occupations, professions and organizations before joining
Appraisal interview – session where supervisor provides feedback of employees on past performance
Aptitude tests – measures what a person is capable of learning
Area of job freedom – area of discretion over job
Arbitrator – neutral third-party who resolves disputes
Assessment center – process where individuals are evaluated to see if they have the skills needed for a job
Assertive style – expressive and does not take unfair advantage
Assimilation – minority members must learn ways of majority
Assumed similarity – the assumption that others are like oneself
At-risk pay – pay not received if employee does not meet targets
Attitude – a frame of mind that predisposes a reaction (three components: thoughts, feelings, behavior)
Attribution theory – explains how we judge people differently based on the attribute we give their behavior
Attribution – judgments on behavior
Augmented skills – skills helpful to expatriate managers
Authoritarianism – power and status exist in an organization
Authority – the right to tell people what to do

Authorization card – statement signed by employee empowering union to negotiate on their behalf
Autocratic leader – leader who centralizes authority to self
Autocratic model – management view that power and authority are necessary to control employees
Autonomy – degree to which a job gives freedom, independence, scheduling and procedures
Avoidance (negative reinforcement) – avoiding or escaping unpleasant stimuli with acceptable behaviors

B

Baseline information – existing operation levels used to compare
Bases of power – sources of power that leaders use (personal, legitimate, expert, reward and coercive)
BATNA – acronym for Best Alternative to a Negotiated Agreement (Fisher and Ury), alternative action that will be taken should agreement with another party not materialize; if the potential results of your current negotiation only offers a value that is less than your BATNA, there is no point in proceeding with the negotiation, and one should use their best available alternative option instead
Behavioral bias – narrow point of view emphasizing satisfying employees; overlooking broader system of organization
Behavioral component – attitude referring to behavior
Behavioral intentions – employee plans to act in a certain way (e.g., resign, slow down, leave early)
Behavior modification – changing based on reinforcement
Behavioral observation scale (BOS – measures frequency of observed behavior
Behavioral style – decision making style focuses on intuition and has a low tolerance for ambiguity
Behaviorally anchored rating scale (BARS – rating technique that judges an employee's performance on job
Benchmarking – process of measuring products, services, and practices against competitors
Big five model – five-factor personality model that includes; extraversion, agreeableness, conscientiousness, emotional stability, and openness to experience

Biofeedback – people learn from feedback to influence systems of stress through medical equipment
Blog – online journal
Boiled frog phenomenon – small changes are unnoticed (a frog will stay in a pot of water as it slowly comes to a boil)
Boundary spanners – employees with strong communication skills within and outside their group
Bounded rationality – people only have time to process a certain amount of information
Brainstorming – group encouraging creative and quick thinking without judgment or evaluation of ideas
Bureaucratic control – control based on rules and hierarchy
Bureaucratic organization – classical management of authority, records and separation of management and ownership
Burnout – most severe stage of distress characterized by lack or productivity, depression and frustration

C

Case study – in-depth study of situation, group or organization
Causal attribution – suspected causes of behavior
Centralization – authority in a central location
Centralized network – team communication where team members communicate through a spokesperson
Certainty – degree that all outcomes are known
Chain of command – unbroken line of authority
Chain reaction effect – a change directly affecting one or a few may lead to a reaction from many due to mutual interest
Change agent – someone who organizes change
Change and acquisition – employees must master tasks and roles to adjust to work values and norms
Channel – the communication carrier
Channel richness – the amount of information that can be transmitted during a communication episode
Charismatic leader – leaders with the ability to motivate
Chief ethics officer – executive over ethics in an organization
Child ego state – psychological position from demonstration of emotions developed based on childhood experiences
Clan culture – focus on values rather than stability and control

Classical perspective of management – emphasizes rational, scientific approach to management
Clarified thinking – thinking without emotion (only rational)
Closed system – a self-sufficient entity
Cluster chain – grapevine (gossip) chain
Coach – style where leader supports team but does not engage
Coalition – informal alliance
Code of ethics – formal statement of values
Codetermination – representation of labor on board of directors of an organization
Coercive power – derived from authority to punish
Cognitive component – part of attitude make up of beliefs, opinions, and knowledge
Cognitive dissonance – psychological discomfort when attitudes and behaviors are inconsistent
Cohesiveness – degree which group members get along
Collectivism – idea that people take care of each other (harmony)
Collegial model – management view of teamwork to motivate
Committee – long lasting team that meets regularly with authority over a task/problem
Communication – transfer of information between people
Communication overload – receives more data than can process
Comparable worth – concept that jobs that are not similar but equal in terms of value be paid equally
Compensation – monetary and non-monetary rewards for work
Compensatory model – selection decision where a high score in one area can compensate for a low score in another
Competence based pay – pay based on employee's skill
Competence motivation – drive to excel
Competency assessment – analysis of the skills needed for knowledge intensive jobs
Competitive advantage – factors that set an organization apart
Competitive intelligence – knowledge of who the competition is and their core competencies (environmental scanning)
Complementary transaction – communication where ego states of sender and receiver in opening are reversed in response
Complete pay program – special pay to realize varied objectives (e.g., retention, recruitment, production, teamwork)
Compressed workweek – staff works longer with shorter weeks

Conceptual skill – ability to think in terms of models, frameworks and broad relationships

Conditional strokes – offered to employees if they perform and avoid problems

Conflict – disagreement, one party believes another is opposing its interests

Conformity – norm of others rules (no independent thinking)

Confronting – facing a conflict to resolve

Consensus – agreement

Consideration – concern over employee and human needs

Construct validity – extent which selection test measures a trait

Constructive discharge – employee resigns because of unreasonable employment conditions

Consultative management – employees encouraged to think of issues and solutions before decisions are made

Content theories – emphasize the needs that motivate

Content validity – extent which selection instrument adequately assesses knowledge and skills

Contingency factors – variables that influence leadership style

Continuous improvement – constant small changes to improve

Continuous reinforcement schedule – reinforcing every desired behavior

Contrast error – rating error on an evaluation due to employee being compared to previous evaluation

Controlling – management function that monitors, assesses and corrects performance

Cooperative training – combination of on the job training with formal education classes

Core competence – organization's specialty

Core dimensions – five factors of job skills (skill variety, task identity, task significance, autonomy and feedback)

Corrective discipline – actions that discourage further infractions

Cost-benefit analysis – determining net effects of actions based on positive and negative

Cost leadership – organization seeks efficiency and tight cost controls to be more efficient than the competition

Cost-reward comparison – employees compare personal costs and rewards to determine where they feel equality

Counseling – discussion of emotional problems to help cope

Counseling functions – six aspects of counseling (advice, reassurance, communication, releasing emotional tension, clarified thinking and reorientation)
Counterproductive work behaviors (CWBs) – behavior that harms employee or organization
Creativity – developing something unique
Credibility gap – difference between what person says and does
Criterion related validity – extent which selection tool predicts important work behavior elements
Critical incident – event that denotes superior or inferior employee performance
Critical incident method – important tasks identified for success
Cross-cultural training – experiences that help someone adjust to a new country/culture
Cross-functional team – groups of employees from different departments cooperating for a single goal
Cross training – training employees in related jobs (rotation)
Cross validation – verifying results of one test with the results from a different test
Crossed transaction – communication where stimulus lines from opening are not parallel in response
Cultural contingency – most productive organizational practices rely on the cultural location of the organization
Cultural distance – difference between two social systems
Cultural diversity – using differences in a positive way
Cultural empathy – awareness of differences in relations
Cultural intelligence – identify cultural signals correctly
Cultural leader – manager that uses symbols to influence culture
Culture shock – feeling of confusion and disorientation when submersed in a different culture
Custodial model – perspective that security needs dominate
Customer appraisal – performance appraisal based on TQM seeking evaluation from internal and external environment

D

Data – unanalyzed facts and figures
Decentralization – power is dispersed in an organization
Decision-making model of leadership – leadership style to match results with one of five leadership options (Vroom)

Decision tree – graphical representation of decision-making
Decruitment – techniques for reducing labor supply within the organization (layoffs, firings, transfers, and job sharing)
Deep acting – modifying inner feelings through conscious effort
Defense mechanism – emotional blocks to protect self
Defensive reasoning – communication used by people about to lose a conflict inappropriately blaming others
Deferred judgment – holding off evaluation of ideas until later
Delegation – transferring authority to lower tiers in organization
Delphi decision group – questionnaires used and group members do not meet in-person (good for physical distance)
Democratic leader – delegates and encourages participation, relies on expert and referent power to manage
Departmentalization – basis of which groups are divided into departments in an organization
Depression – negative emotion associated with gloom, sadness, and loss of interest in normal activities
Developmental relationship strength – quality of network relationships
Devil's advocate – decision-making technique where an individual is assigned the role of challenging assumptions
Diagnosis – step in decision-making which the management analyzes the causal factors for a situation
Dialectic decision model (DDM) – examining two or more proposals by subgroups for whole-group decision (debate)
Directive counseling – listening, resolving and directing
Directive style – decision-making style that focuses on rationality with a low tolerance for ambiguity
Disabled individual – physical or mental impairment, record of the impairment, and is regarded as having the impairment
Discharge – separation of employee from company for a cause
Discipline – punishment or orderly behavior in an organization or training that molds and strengthens
Discrimination – biased treatment based on criteria not relevant
Disparate treatment – protected class has a different evaluation system than a non-protected class
Distributive justice – perceived fairness
Distress – harmful stress characterized by feelings of inadequacy
Division of work – levels of authority and functional units

Double-loop learning – using current information about change to better prepare employees for future changes
Downsizing – planned elimination of jobs
Downward communication – messages from management to staff
Drive – motivation for affiliation, power, or competence
Due process – employee's right to present their position
Dysfunctional effect – poor impact of an action or change

E

e-business – running an entire business online (e.g., Amazon)
Earnings at-risk incentives – puts some employee's pay at risk, but gives them a chance to earn extra pay
Ecological control – altering environment to influence others
Economic forces – culture that guides the resources
Economic incentive system – altering pay based on individual, group or organizational performance
Effectiveness – degree that an organization achieves its goals
Efficiency – degree that an organization achieves its goals with less resources
Ego states – psychological position of parent, adult or child that guide social interaction
Ego strength – degree of strength in a person's convictions
Electronic monitoring – technological surveillance of behavior
Emotional catharsis – release of emotion through telling someone
Emotional intelligence – self-manage and interact constructively
Emotional labor – employee's expression of organizationally desired emotions during interpersonal transactions at work
Employee assistance programs (EAP – programs that help employees work through personal problems
Employee involvement groups – group of employees that meet in an attempt to resolve problems
Employee ownership – program where employees provide capital to purchase control over an operation
Employee teams – work functions are divided into groups (in lieu of individuals) and team is given self-management
Employment at will principle – the right of an employer to fire an employee without a reason

Empowerment – delegation of power to subordinates
Enacted values – values exhibited by employees
Encounter phase – employees come to terms with expectations and what organization is really like
Enriched sociotechnical work system – most of organization is built into a balanced human-technical system
Enterprise resource planning (ERP) – unites all the business functions in an organization
Environmental scanning – assessing the outside environment and what affects it may have on the organization
Equal employment opportunity (EEO – treatment of individuals is fair
Equal Pay Act of 1963 – reward systems same despite gender
Equity sensitivity – employee tolerance for equity
Equity theory – examines people's perceptions of equality
ERG theory – simplified hierarchy theory: existence, relatedness, and growth (developed by Alderfer)
Escalating commitment – continuous outlay in bad decisions
Espoused values – values and norms preferred by organization
Ethical dilemma – situation where all choices are undesirable
Ethical imperative – belief that participation is needed in decisions for moral reasons
Ethical leadership – based on moral integrity (e.g., social responsibility, open communication and cost-benefit)
Ethics – moral values
Ethnocentrism – belief that one culture group is better
Ethnorelativism – belief that culture groups are equal
Eustress – good stress that motivates someone to do better
Existence needs – physiological and security factors
Exit interview – interview with exit employees to find out why
Expatriates – live and work in a different country than own
Expectancy model – motivations depend on people's expectations of rewards (valence, expectancy and instrumentality)
Expert power – power that comes from special knowledge of the tasks of their subordinates
Experiential learning – learn by experience in training environment the kinds of problems faced on the job
Explicit knowledge – information that is easily put into words
External factors – environmental characteristics that influence

External locus of control – person's belief that outcomes are beyond their control (e.g., fate)
External organizational environment – factors that exist outside the organization that impact it
Extinction – eliminating behavior by ignoring or not reinforcing
Extranet – company communications that gives access to the organizations they do business with (externally)
Extrinsic reward – reward given by another

F

Facilitators – process consultants to examine team roles
Fact premises – views based on research and experience
Failure rate – percentage of expatriates who are unsatisfactory
Fair employment practices – state and local laws governing equal employment opportunity
Fast-track program – quick promotions to young managers with high potential
Feedback – objective information about performance
Femininity – decision making that focuses on life-quality
Field study – evaluation of real-life variables
Filtering – reducing communication to basics to be passed on
First mover – organization that is first to bring some sort of innovation to the market
First-line managers – lowest level managers
Flat structure – few hierarchies of power
Flexible benefits – allow employees to choose benefits that meet their needs, most popular are modular (meets needs of a specific group), core plus (essential benefits with a menu selection of other options), and flexible spending (set aside dollar amounts for services like childcare and healthcare)
Flextime – scheduling freedom for employees as long as they put the same amount of hours in
Followership – traits that help a person be a good subordinate
Forced-choice method – performance appraisal method that requires rater to choose from statements that distinguishes between satisfactory and unsatisfactory performance
Force-field analysis – evaluating change forces (drive or inhibit)
Formal team – team created by organization

Formal communication channel – communication defined by chain of command
Forming – group stage characterized by acquaintance
Framing – the way a question is asked or language used to influence another's perception
Free-rein leader – leader that avoids power and responsibility
Free rider – person that does less work in a team but receives the same benefits
Frustration-regression principle – idea that if one need is not met the individual will regress to a lower need
Functional job analysis – quantitative job analysis that evaluates data, people, and things
Functional conflict – serves organization interests
Fundamental attribution error – underestimate external factors; successes are good luck and failures are flaws

G

Gainsharing plans – programs that share the financial gains based on a formula that reflects productivity
Garbage can model – belief that decision-making is sloppy
General adaptation syndrome (GAS) – stress cycle; alarm, resistance, exhaustion
Genetic monitoring – identification of harmful substances in workplace for corrective action
Geocentric organizations – ignore nationality when integrating community of interest
Glass ceiling – invisible barriers for minorities and women
Global outsourcing – using foreign labor to save money
Global team – culturally diverse work team
Goal – desired future state
Grand strategy – plan to achieve long-term goals
Grapevine – informal communication channel (gossip)
Group decision support system – technology removing communication barriers decision processes within a group
Group support systems (GSSs) – computer software that helps people work better together
Groupthink – conformity agreement without critical evaluation
Growth need – need for self-esteem and actualization

H

Halo effect – general assumptions based on a few traits
Hay profile method – job evaluation that uses knowledge, mental activity, and accountability to evaluate
Hero – person in organization that embodies the values
Heuristics – rules of thumb
Hidden agendas – private motives of group members
Hierarchy culture – internal focus and values stability and control over flexibility
Hierarchy of needs theory – five ascending categories of needs physiological, safety, social, esteem and self-actualization
High context culture – people use situational cues to develop portrait of person
Higher-order needs – Maslow's top three needs (social, esteem and actualization)
Holistic OB – evaluating whole person, organization or group
Homeostasis – self-correcting mechanism to restore balance
Honesty tests – assessing employee integrity
Horizontal communication – communication among peers
Host country – country where an international company operates
Host country nationals – people who are natives to the host country and work in the organization
Hot stove rule – discipline warning, effective, enforced consistently, and applies to all employees fairly
Human capital – employees' skills, capabilities, and experience
Human resource approach – activities to attract, develop, and retain a good staff (also known as *supportive approach*)
Human skill – ability of a person to work with others
Humanistic perspective – management perspective emphasizing the workers needs
Humility – giving credit to others when recognizing success
Hygiene factors – satisfy workers when they exist and dissatisfy in their absence but existence is not motivating

I

Iceberg model of counseling – recognizes there are more to feelings that lie beneath surface
Idea champion – someone who starts change in an organization

Idea incubator – in-house safe-house for ideas for change
Illusory correlation – association of two events, when there is no real connection
Immediate corrective action – corrective actions used once to quickly get performance back up to par
Implementation – putting a plan into action
Imposter phenomenon – belief that abilities are not as great as others perceive
Impression management – getting others to view in certain way; high self-monitors likely to engage, molding image to fit situation (e.g., conforming, apologizing, self-promotion, flattery, favors, association)
Incentives – environmental factors used to motivate
Individualism approach – if the act will be the best in the long run for the individual, then it is moral
Individualistic culture – emphasis on personal freedom/choice
Individualization – employees exerting influence on social system
Industrial democracy – worker participating at various levels of the organization for decisions affecting workers
Inference – interpretation based on symbols (not facts)
Informal group – formed by friends
Informal leaders – person with largest amount of status in an informal group that emerges to exhibit influence
Informal organization – network of social relations not established or required that happen as people associate
Information – data converted to meaning
In-group exchange – partnership of trust, respect and admiration
Initiating structure – organizing and defining group roles
Institutionalization – when the organization takes on a life of its own (apart from its founders or members)
Instrumentality – belief in reward receipt upon completion
Intelligence – ability to think, reason and solve problems
Interactional justice – perceived fairness by decision-makers
Interactive leadership – leader seen as caring and collaborative
Intermittent reinforcement – rewarding some instances of a desired behavior
Internal factors – personal characteristics that cause behavior
Internal locus of control – belief that self is responsible for actions (e.g., will)

International corporation – domestic organization that moves into foreign countries
International dimension – external environment that represents events in foreign environments affecting the organization
Interventions – structured activities to improve effectiveness
Intranet – internal communications system
Intrinsic reward – pleasurable feeling someone gets from conducting an activity (motivated from the inside)
Intuition – unconscious apprehension

J

Jargon – language or terms specific to a job or organization
Job analysis – determining duties, tasks, and responsibilities
Job breadth – different tasks an individual is responsible for
Job characteristics model – job design that supports meaningfulness, responsibility, and knowledge, five core dimensions are; skill variety, task identity, task significance, autonomy, feedback
Job classification system – jobs grouped into wage grades
Job content – conditions related to job and performance
Job context – conditions related to environment and performance
Job description – statement of tasks, expectations, and duties
Job depth – amount of control responsibility and discretion employee has over how job is performed
Job design – improves jobs through technological or human considerations to improve productivity and satisfaction
Job diagnostics survey – presence of five core dimensions
Job enlargement – making a job more challenging
Job enrichment Error! Bookmark not defined. – making a job more meaningful
Job family – group of individual but similar jobs
Job involvement – how an employee immerses self in the job (investment of time) and how central it is in their lives
Job rotation – moves employees to different jobs for variety
Job satisfaction – positive attitude toward a job
Job scope – assessment of job breadth and depth to determine room for enlargement or enrichment
Job simplification – making a job less challenging

Job specification – statement of needed skills, knowledge and abilities for the position
Judgmental heuristics – rules of thumb used to reduce information processing demands
Justice approach – moral decisions are fair and impartial
Just-in-time training – employees given key information in small increments when needed

K

Kaizen – belief that people should improve everything
Knowledge management – organize/accessibility of knowledge
Knowledge workers – job extends beyond physical position to plan, decision-making, and problem solving

L

Laissez-fair style – leader who gives control to the group
Lateral communication – communication across chains of command
Law of diminishing returns – declining amount of extra output received when more of a desirable input is added
Law of effect – behavior with positive consequences is repeated, and negative ones are not
Law of individual differences – belief that people are different
Layoff survivor's sickness – feeling guilt, anger and distrust following layoff of co-workers
Leader-member exchange model – leaders and followers exchange information and role expectations determine the quality of the interpersonal relationships
Leader-member relations – degree leader is accepted by group
Leader-position power – power granted by position
Leadership – ability to influence
Leadership style – leader's skills, traits and attitudes
Learned helplessness – employees act dependent and have no faith in their own abilities
Learning capabilities – core competencies and processes that allow an organization to adapt

Learning organization – everyone engaged in solving problems and improve the organization, proactively creates, acquires and transfers knowledge throughout organization
Legal/political dimension – general environment in laws and regulations that influence an organization
Legitimate power – power given by the organization
Liaison individuals – active in grapevine
Life position – dominant characteristics that remain unless a major experience alters
Line authority – power to direct and control subordinates
Linguistics – speaking pattern
Linking pin – manager's role of group connection to organization
Listening – receiving messages to understand what is being said
Long-term orientation – value of preparing for future
Loose rates – payment allowing employees to reach standard output with limited effort
Low context culture – reliance on literal and written cues
Lower-order needs – the physiological and safety/security needs in Maslow's hierarchy
Lump-sum merit program – employees receive a year-end payment that is not added to their base salary

M

Machiavellianism – manipulating others for power/personal gain
Macromotivation – factors outside an organization that influence employee's performance
Maintenance roles – relationship building group behavior
Management – attaining organizational goals by planning, leading, and controlling the organization
Management by objectives (MBO) – rates performance on achievement of goals set by mutual agreement (Drucker)
Management by walking around (MBWA) – communication where managers interact with workers
Managerial grid – framework of management styles based on concern for people and production
Managing diversity – being aware of characteristic differences of employees and managing people as individuals
Market culture – values stability and control with external focus
Masculinity – focus on achievement and assertiveness

Matrix organization – two chains of command for employees due to different types of organizational structure
Mechanistic organization – uses hierarchy, centralization, task certainty and role definition
Mediation – third party resolution to conflict
Melting pot – assumption that people want to assimilate
Mentor – experienced person teaching less experienced person
Micromotivation – factors inside the organization that affect an employee's productivity
Middle-management committees – groups that improve participation and communication below the top level
Mission – reason for an organization to exist
Mission statement – defines the reason for organization
Monochronic time – preference for doing one thing at a time because time is limited (schedule driven)
Monoculture – accepts only one set of values and beliefs
Morale – job satisfaction and happiness
Moral-rights approach – moral decisions are ones that retain the individual's moral rights
Motivating potential score (MPS) – degree that a job is associated with meaning and responsibility
Motivation – direction to accomplish something
Motivational factors – motivating when they exist but their absence is not usually dissatisfying
Multinational organization – operate in more than one country
Mutuality of interest – idea that organizations and people are interdependent and should create mutual goals

N

Natural work module – job designed to create entire product
Natural work team – group of employees that produce a product
Need for achievement – desire to do something difficult
Need for affiliation – desire to be accepted by peers
Need for power – desire to influence others
Negative inequity – receive greater outcomes for same inputs
Negative reinforcement – encouraging behavior by withdrawing something negative
Negative strokes – recognition of pain (physical or emotion) and detracts for other's feelings of satisfactory

Negotiation – compromise between two or more parties
Neighborhoods of offices – centers of individual offices arranged to form social groups
Nepotism – hiring of relatives over current employees
Network – group of people that exchange information about shared interests
Network charts – informal organization charts
Networking – making contacts with groups of people
Neutralizer – variable that offsets leadership style
Nominal group technique (NGT) – idea generating process
Nonanalytic – ready-made rules to make decisions
Nonassertive style – timid behavior
Nondirective counseling – listening, encouraging and helping determine solutions to problems
Nonparticipator role – team member that contributes little
Nonprogrammed decision – responsive situation-based decision
Nonrational models – models of how a decision was reached
Nonverbal communication – communications transmitted in a form other than words
Norm – standard of conduct
Norm of reciprocity – two people in a relationship feel need to repay social debts to each other
Normative commitment – employee's obligation to remain with an organization for ethical reasons
Norming – stage of team development where conflicts are resolved and unity becomes prevalent

O

Ombudsman – individual designated to receive complaints and resolution from employees
Omnipotent view of management – managers are responsible for success or failure
On-the-job training (OJT) – training conducted as the employee is learning from a more experienced person on the job
Onboarding – program to help employee integrate in a new job
Open-book management – open sharing of financial information
Open-door policy – settling grievances through various levels of management (not necessarily exact chain of command)

Open-end questions – questions allowing the answerer to respond with their feelings or thoughts
Open system – encouraging environment interaction through boundaries, inputs and outputs
Operant behavior – learned behavior through consequences
Organic organization – fluid and flexible group
Organization – structured entity with a goal
Organization analysis – examination of environment, strategies, and resources of an organization
Organization-based self-esteem – how important a worker perceives self to the organization
Organization chart – visual depiction of organizational structure
Organizational behavior – a behavioral science that explores individuals and groups in organizations
Organizational citizenship – work behavior that is beyond job requirements that contribute to its success
Organizational commitment – loyalty to an organization
Organizational control – process which managers regulate the activities to make them consistent with goals
Organizational development (OD) – behavioral science that targets effectiveness of organization (planned change)
Organizational learning curve for change – adaptation period after change (declined effectiveness until equilibrium)
Organizational politics – self-interest motivated behaviors
Organizational socialization – process where employees' learn of the organization's culture
Orientation – introduction to organization's rules and regulations
Ostracism – alienation by other group members
Out-group exchange – partnership shrouded in distrust
Outcomes – reward employees receive
Output restriction – choose to produce less than able
Outsourcing – finding outside people to perform jobs that were done inside the organization
Overparticipation – staff has more participation than want

P

Paradigms – explanations of how things work
Parent ego state – psychological reaction that is critical, nurturing, controlling, instructive or protective

Parochialism – only able to see situation from self-perspective
Partial reinforcement schedule – some occurrences rewarded
Participative counseling – mutual exchange of ideas to help person solve problems
Participative leaders – decentralization of authority by consultation with staff
Participative management – programs that empower employees by involving them with the decision-making
Path-goal theory – contingency approach where leadership is responsible for clarifying rewards and consequences
Pay equity – perception that pay is in equal value to work
Pay for performance – compensation based on job performance
Perceived control – control an employee thinks they have
Perception – self-interpretation of the environment
Perceptual set – tendency to perceive what was expected
Perceptual defense – protection by ignoring threatening concepts
Perceptual distortion – inaccuracies in perception
Perceptual selectivity – people select what to pay attention to
Performance appraisal – evaluation on performance
Performance gap – difference between performance expectation and actual performance
Performance-satisfaction-effort loop – flow model showing relationship between performance, satisfaction and effort
Performing – team development stage focused is on goal
Personal barriers – communication interference due to emotion, poor listening or values
Personal power – comes from strength of personality
Personal wellness – programs of preventative maintenance
Personality – characteristics that dictate behavior
Physical withdrawal – early departures, arriving late and unauthorized absences to retaliate
Piecework – work paid by the number produced
Point-counterpoint – decision-making technique where people are assigned the expression of competing points of view
Polarization – extreme differences in beliefs
Political power – derived from allegiance and support
Polychronic time – preference to do more than one thing at once because time is flexible
Positive discipline – focuses on early correction of misconduct with the employee correcting the problem

Positive inequity – other person lesser outcomes for same inputs
Positive reinforcement – rewarding behavior
Positive strokes – consequence that feels good and encourages others sense of contentment
Post-traumatic stress disorder – stressful consequences of a traumatic event
Power distance – degree of inequality acceptance from individuals in the organization
Preventative discipline – actions that pare preemptively taken to discourage infractions
Primary needs – basic physiological and security needs
Primary outcomes – rewards employees receive directly following actions
Proactive change – anticipating events and taking control
Procedural justice – perceived fairness of the procedures used to make a decision
Profit sharing – employer pays deferred sums based on the profits of the company
Programmed conflict – encourages difference of opinion to reach best decision
Programmed decision – choice made about a situation that has recurred so the decision-maker can rely on past choices
Progressive discipline – stronger penalties for more infractions
Proxemics – feelings about interpersonal space across cultures
Psychic costs – costs that affect a person's psyche
Psychological contract – unwritten agreement about what an employee expects to give and receive from the system
Psychological distance – emotional separation
Punishment – unfavorable consequence to stop behavior

Q

Quality circle – voluntary group of 6-12 that meet regularly to discuss organizational issues
Quality of life – emphasizes relationship to others
Quantity of life – emphasizes assertiveness, money and goods
Quick fixes – fads that fix symptoms but not the problem

R

Range of variation – acceptable difference of expectations and actual output
Rate setting – determination of standard output per job
Rational model – four-step approach to decisions
Reactive change – change when outside factors have already influenced performance
Readiness – followers' ability and willingness to participate
Realistic job preview (RJP) – informing applicants about the job (even undesirable portions of it)
Reasonable accommodation – changes made for disabled people or people of a different religion to perform a job
Recency error – error in appraisal to base all of factors on employee's most recent behavior
Reference group – group norms that a person accepts
Referent power – derived of characteristics commanding subordinates' identification (respect and admiration)
Refreezing – after change in an organization the new standards, policies, and processes are cemented
Reinforcement schedule – frequency which reinforcement accompanies behavior (continuous, fixed-interval, fixed-ratio, variable-interval, variable-ratio)
Reliability – degree which interviews and tests give a predictable result of job performance
Repatriation – employee returns home from international
Respondent behavior – unlearned stimulus-response reflexes
Retraining – allowing employees to learn new skills with technological advances that have changed their jobs
Reverse culture shock – expatriates' difficulty in re-adjusting
Reverse discrimination – preferences to protected classes to extent that unprotected classes are discriminated
Reward power – authority to reward others
Rights of privacy – freedom from organizational control into private life and release of confidential information
Risk propensity – individual's willingness to accept risk
Risky shift – group becomes more risky when resources are not their own and will not be held accountable individually
Role – set of expectations of behavior

Role conflict – incompatible roles in the organization

S

Sabbatical leave – time off for stress relief or education
Sample survey – questionnaire from a sampling of people
Sanctions – rewards and penalties groups use to establish norms
Satisficing – applying first suitable decision even if it not optimal
Scenario technique – speculative tool identifying future states if conditions are met
Schema – mental picture
Secondary needs – social and psychological needs
Secondary outcomes – rewards received indirectly following primary outcomes
Selective perception – paying attention to factors that reinforce self-expectations
Self-actualization – highest need to become what capable of
Self-appraisal – performance appraisal that is completed on self-performance prior to formal appraisal
Self-concept – self-perception physically, spiritually and emotionally
Self-efficacy – internal belief of abilities to perform
Self-fulfilling prophecy – (Pygmalion effect) meeting high or low expectations of others
Self-management teams – group given oversight authority
Self-monitoring – observing self-behavior and adapting
Self-serving bias – overestimate internal factors to success
Semantic barriers – communication limitations caused by various meanings of words or symbols
Sense of choice – ability to use judgment on task
Sense of competence – high-quality work
Sense of meaningfulness – completing something meaningful
Sense of progress – pride in accomplishing something important
Servant leader – leader who puts subordinate needs before own
Sexual harassment – unwelcome advances, requests, and verbal or physical sexual contact
Shaping – reinforcing closer and closer behaviors until the ultimate goal is acquired
Short-circuiting – skipping steps in communication hierarchy

Short-term orientation – value on past and accenting present with respect to tradition, historical and social obligations
Silver handshake – early retirement incentive with a bonus or increased retirement benefits
Similar to me error – appraisal error where the appraiser inflates the evaluation because they are personable
Single-loop learning – process of solving immediate issues and adapting to change from employees
Situation analysis – evaluation of the strengths, weakness, opportunities, and threats
Situational theories – leadership style should match situation
Skill-based pay – pay based on knowledge
Skill inventories – files of knowledge, skills, and abilities of employees so management can quickly fill openings
Skunkworks – team, usually secretive, that focuses on innovation
Social capital – potential of strong social relationships
Social cues – information (positive or negative) that employees receive from social network that influence behavior
Social desirability bias – changing answers based on thoughts of what society wants
Social equilibrium – balance of interdependent parts of a system
Social facilitation – trying harder because people are present
Social forces – culture in an organization that guides the relationships with the people
Social information processing – recognizing that social cues affect perceptions
Social leader – person who maintains group relationships
Social learning theory – belief that learned behavior is through observing and imitating role models (also known as social cognitive theory or self-efficacy)
Social loafing – individuals apply less effort in a team
Social responsibility – obligation for organization to better society
Sociocultural dimension – general environment that represents demographics
Socioeconomic model of decision making – considers social costs/benefits as well as economic and technical values
Socioemotional role – role in a group where the member focuses on the team's emotional needs
Span of management – number of employees per supervisor

Spillover effect – relationship between job and life satisfaction
Spot bonus – unplanned bonus given to an employee for effort
Staff authority – authority granted to staff in their specialty
Stages of team development – group evolution stages; forming, storming, norming, performing and (at times) adjourning
Standard hour plan – rewards for completion in a specific time
Status – social rank
Status anxiety – upset over difference of status and desired status
Status deprivation – loss of status
Status symbols – visible items that show importance
Step review system – reviewing employee grievances by successively going to higher levels of management
Stereotyping – judging someone based on a few characteristics
Storming – team stage characterized by conflict as individual personalities emerge and power is determined
Straight commission plan – pay based on sale percentage
Straight piecework – pay per unit produced
Strategic constituency – group of people with stake in an organization's success
Strategic plans – steps needed to reach strategic goals
Stress – life pressures
Stress-performance model – depiction of relationship between stress and performance (different thresholds for people)
Stress threshold – level of stress that can be tolerated
Stressors – conditions that cause pressure
Stroking – recognition
Structure – management focus on task orientation (sometimes at the sake of personal issues and emotions)
Subordinate appraisal – appraisal of a supervisor by an employee (usually used for development purposes)
Substitutes for leadership – factors that reduce the need for leadership behaviors
Succession planning – identifying people for successive positions
Superleadership – encourage employee self-leadership
Superordinate goal – goals that need collaboration
Supportive approach to OB – working with people to satisfy both their needs and growth potential
Supportive model – supports growth and development
Surface acting – hiding inner feelings with facial expressions

Surface agenda – official group tasking
Synergy – the whole is greater than the sum of the parts
Symbolic view of management – outside factors responsible for the success or failure (opposite of omnipotent view)
Systems approach to OB – variables in an organization affect each other

T

Tacit knowledge – experiential knowledge that is hard to express
Tall structure – many hierarchies within the organization
Task analysis – determination of content of a training program based on the tasks of a job
Task conflict – conflicts over goals and content of work
Task environment – external environment affecting the organizations operations
Task identity – allowing employee to complete a piece of work
Task leaders – person helping group accomplish goals
Task specialist role – role in a group where the member focuses on the task given to the group
Team – small group with complementary skills
Team incentive plan – incentive pay for team when they have met or exceeded standards
Telecommuting (telework) – working from remote location through technology
Theory X– people are basically lazy and must be coerced to work
Theory Y– people like to work and can exercise self-direction
Theory Z – Japanese management to U.S. culture highlighting cooperation and consensus
Total quality management – focuses on total organization by involvement, benchmarking and improvement
Training multiplier effect – skilled people develop others, who then develop others
Trait – characteristic
Transactional leader – clarifies roles and initiates structure, provides rewards, and shows consideration
Transfer – moving an employee laterally in the organization
Transfer of training – effectively using the skills learned in training on the job
Transformational leader – ability to bring change

Triple-reward system – rewards that benefits employees, organization and social system
Tunnel vision – narrow viewpoints
Turnover – amount of people that leave an organization
Two-factor model of motivation – motivator factors motivate and hygiene factors dissatisfy in absence (Herzberg)
Two-way communication process – eight-step process of communication (develop, encode, transmit, receive, decode, accept, use, feedback)
Type A personality – extreme competitiveness, impatience, aggression, and work devotion
Type B personality – balanced, relaxed, and laid back lifestyle

U

Uncertainty avoidance – people's intolerance for ambiguity
Unconditional strokes – strokes without behavior connection
Underparticipation – employees want more participation
Unfair labor practices (ULPs – practices that deny a person their rights under the federal labor laws
Unfreezing – before change takes place the current organizational ways are unfrozen
Unity of command – employees should report to one manager
Upward communication – sent from subordinates to superiors
Upward feedback – employees provide feedback on supervisors
Utilitarian approach – the greatest good to the greatest amount of people is a moral decision

V

Valence – value individual has on an outcome
Validity – degree that correctly measures what it is meant to
Value added compensation – payment program for advancing the needs of employees and goals of the organization
Value attainment – job allows fulfillment of values
Value premises – personal views of how desirable a goal is
Variable pay – pay linked to performance
Virtual team – team linked via electronic means
Vision – ideal future of an organization

W

Wage and salary survey – survey of wages paid to employees by other employers in the same labor market
Wage curve – graphical representation of the relationship between worth of job and wage
Wage incentive – pay more for more production
Wage rate compensation – differential between job classes (hourly workers and managers)
Whistle-blowing – when an employee tells about illegal or illegitimate practices
Withdrawal cognitions – overall thoughts about quitting job
Work permit – government document authorizing employment of foreign individual
Workforce utilization analysis – classifying protected-class workers by the number and types of jobs in an organization
Workplace spirituality – recognizes desire for meaningful work with community and strong sense of purpose, focuses on individual development, trust and respect, humanistic work practices and toleration of expression

X

Xenophobia – rejection and fear of different ideas

Practice Test

1. The degree of which people accept inequality is called:
   a. Individualism
   b. Masculinity
   c. Power distance
   d. Uncertainty avoidance

Use the following for questions 2-5

A. Competing
B. Avoiding
C. Compromising
D. Accommodating

2. Conflict management technique when issue is unimportant.

3. Conflict management using assertiveness.

4. Conflict management technique used when someone knows he/she is wrong or the issue is not as important.

5. Conflict management technique used when both parties have equal power.

6. What is the continuous investment in a poor decision called?
   a. Escalating commitment
   b. Groupthink
   c. Group avoidance
   d. Slippery slope

7. __________ is the removal of something unpleasant following a desired behavior.
   a. Positive reinforcement
   b. Negative reinforcement
   c. Punishment
   d. Extinction

Use the following for questions 8-11

A. ERG Theory
B. Theory X and Theory Y
C. Two-Factor Theory
D. Equity Theory

8. The two components are that either people are very lazy, or they have the ability to self-direct and are creative.

9. The two components are issues that eliminate job dissatisfaction and do not motivate (hygiene) and issues that cause job satisfaction and motivate (motivators).

10. Focuses on three needs (existence, relatedness, and growth).

11. Examines how people strive for perceived fairness by changing inputs, outcomes, distort perception, or exit.

12. Which of the following is true of a learning organization?
    a. Autocratic in problem solving
    b. Celebrates stability and reliability
    c. Focuses on individual versus team work
    d. Empowers employees to take risks be creative

13. _____ identifies the degree that employee performs a job from beginning to ending.
    a. Autonomy
    b. Skill variety
    c. Task identity
    d. Task significance

14. What term describes the tendency for people to apply themselves less in groups?
    a. Social loafing
    b. Groupthink
    c. Oversimplification
    d. Sociological responsibility

15. Decision style relying on significant data and consideration.

a. Directive
b. Analytical
c. Conceptual
d. Behavioral

Use the following for questions 16-19

A. Storming
B. Norming
C. Forming
D. Performing

16. Characterized by conflict

17. Characterized by strong focus on the task at hand

18. Characterized by introduction

19. Characterized by conflict resolution and harmony

20. ________ is a "good enough" approach.

a. Intuition
b. Rationality
c. Bounded rationality
d. Satisficing

Use the following for questions 21-24

A. Legitimate
B. Reward
C. Coercive
D. Expert

21. Power derived from specialized skill/knowledge

22. Power derived from manager's authority to punish

23. Power derived from organizational position

24. Power derived from manager's authority to give incentives

25. _______ is a conflict management technique with third-party engaging in the issue to reach an agreement.

a. Focus on goals
b. Mediation
c. Bargaining/negotiation
d. Renewal strategy

26. The leader expecting the most in the Path-Goal theory.

a. Directive
b. Participative
c. Achievement oriented
d. Supportive

Use the following for questions 27-30

A. Leader
B. Negotiator
C. Spokesperson
D. Entrepreneur

27. Top level manager assigned to find and acquire more business

28. Represents organization at a press conference

29. Visionary and decision-maker that empowers employees

30. In charge of mergers and acquisitions

31. Difference between where an organization is and where they want to be is called a _______:

a. Performance gap
b. Performance break
c. Expectation gap
d. Expectation break

32. The idea that each person has to report to one person

a. Management span
b. Scalar principle
c. Work specialization
d. Unity of command

33. What is the top need on Maslow's Hierarchy of Needs?

a. Physiological
b. Security
c. Belonging
d. Self-actualization

34. What are the five personality factors in the Big Five model?

a. Extraversion, agreeableness, conscientiousness, emotional stability, openness to experience
b. Extraversion, conflict avoidance, ability to empathize, charitable ideas, and adventuresome.
c. Ability to project, conflict avoidance, openness to experience, emotional stability, intelligence
d. Intelligence, creativity, extroversion, conscientiousness, relationships

35. A(n) ___ work/live in a country different than their own.

a. Immigrant
b. Alien
c. Expatriate
d. Refugee

36. ___ is applying something unpleasant for undesired behavior.

a. Punishment
b. Extinction
c. Negative reinforcement
d. Positive reinforcement

37. What is Machiavellianism?

a. Doing whatever is necessary to get to the top
b. People should be collectivist in nature
c. The belief that what happens is due to fate
d. The belief that what happens is due to ambition

38. ______ is reporting unethical or illegal practices of a company.

a. Treason
b. Unethical violation of confidentiality
c. Whistle-blowing
d. Traitorism

39. Which of the following theories involves physiological, safety, belonging, self-esteem, and self self-actualization?
    a. Hawthorne experiments
    b. Maslow's Hierarchy of Needs
    c. Achievement Motivation Theory
    d. Theory X

40. Which of the following is NOT true about goals?
    a. Specific
    b. Measure what means most to a company
    c. Time period should be flexible
    d. Challenging and realistic

41. Which of the following is an example of an intrinsic reward?
    a. Doing a job because the employee likes it
    b. Doing a job because the boss will give a bonus
    c. Doing a job for a positive appraisal performance
    d. Doing a job for a reward

42. Which of the following schools of thought to motivation focuses on economic rewards to motivate performance?
    a. Traditional
    b. Human relations
    c. Human resources
    d. Contemporary

43. The ______ is when someone is rated the same based on just a few attributes.
    a. Contrast error
    b. Similar to me error
    c. Halo effect
    d. Error of central tendency

44. What is eustress?
    a. A type of stress that impacts the heart
    b. A good stress that strives people to accomplish
    c. A bad stress that is harmful
    d. The stress right before burnout (extreme stress)

45. ____ examines how people strive for perceived fairness by changing inputs, outcomes, distort perception or leave the job.

a. ERG
b. Maslow's Hierarchy of Needs
c. Hygiene/Motivators
d. Equity Theory

46. Which of the following theories believes that few people reach the top level of motivation ("transcenders")?

a. McClelland's Acquired Needs Theory
b. Herzberg's Two-Factor Theory
c. McGregor's Theory X and Theory Y
d. Maslow's Hierarchy of Needs Theory

Use the following for questions 47-50

A. Open-door policy
B. Ombudsman system
C. Mediation
D. Step-review system

47. Neutral party hears both sides and renders a compromise.

48. Dispute settlement with various levels of management.

49. Designated employee that others can seek out for counsel.

50. Resolution via successive higher levels of management.

51. Decision based on the greatest good for the greatest quantity:

a. Moral-rights
b. Utilitarian
c. Justice
d. Integrative social theory

52. Decision-making bias based on being influenced by the first (even if irrelevant) information received.

a. Availability heuristic
b. Anchoring bias
c. Confirmation bias
d. Framing bias

Use the following for questions 53-57

A. Job simplification
B. Job enlargement
C. Job rotation
D. Job enrichment

53. Management moves employees to different jobs for variety.

54. Using motivators (e.g., growth) to increase job satisfaction.

55. The improvement of efficiency that is usually resisted.

56. The process of making a job more complex.

Use the following for questions 57-60

A. Punishment
B. Negative reinforcement
C. Positive reinforcement
D. Extinction

57. A monetary bonus for excellent sales is an example of ____.

58. The withdrawal of a reward.

59. The removal of unpleasant stimuli with a desired behavior.

60. Unpleasant stimuli for an undesired behavior.

61. What is task significance?

a. Degree of freedom
b. Degree of variety
c. Degree job is performed from start to finish
d. Perceived importance of a job

62. An ethical school of thought where rights of consent, privacy, conscience, due process, and life must be considered.

a. Justice
b. Utilitarian
c. Moral-rights
d. Individualism

63. Falling productivity in the Equity Theory is an example of?

a. Change outputs
b. Change inputs
c. Distort perceptions
d. Partial reinforcement

64. Which is true with an internal locus of control?

a. They are typically more ethical
b. They believe in fate
c. They have limited accountability for their actions
d. They believe things happen due to luck or chance

65. In the Two-Factor theory pay and working conditions are ___.

a. Hygiene factors
b. Equity
c. Relatedness
d. Motivators

Use the below for questions 66-69

A. Transactional leader
B. Transformational leader
C. Servant leader
D. Charismatic leader

66. Brings innovation by recognizing the needs of employees and looks at new ways to solve existing problems

67. Motivates and inspires vision; is less predictable

68. Prioritizes employees' needs over their own

69. Emphasizes job-oriented needs over personal ones

70. A barrier to perception where someone only processes information that aligns with his/her own beliefs:

a. Selective perception
b. Contrast effects
c. Perception
d. Stereotypes

71. Which model of organizational behavior uses leadership to encourage a common purpose with a strong focus on teamwork?
   a. Autocratic
   b. Custodial
   c. Collegial
   d. Supportive

72. Which of the below is a leadership skill category?
   a. Technical
   b. Human
   c. Conceptual
   d. All of the above

73. Group problem where entire group changes stance to one with more risk:
   a. Groupthink
   b. Social loafing
   c. Groupshift
   d. Punctuated equilibrium

74. Which of the following is NOT true of a goal:
   a. Measurable
   b. Results oriented
   c. General
   d. Time bound

75. Which type of ethical decision stresses that the result must be impartial?
   a. Moral
   b. Justice
   c. Individualism
   d. Integrative social contracts

76. Which stage of creativity focuses on the unconscious?
   a. Incubation
   b. Concentration
   c. Illumination
   d. Verification

77. Common design in large organizations with routine tasks
   a. Matrix
   b. Simple structure
   c. Bureaucracy
   d. None of the above

78. How is organizational culture created?
   a. Purposeful selection
   b. Indoctrination and socialization
   c. Role modeling
   d. All of the above

79. Which is NOT one of Lewin's stages of a planned change?
   a. Unfreezing
   b. Changing
   c. Refreezing
   d. Evaluation

80. Listening style that focuses on main points.
   a. Comprehensive
   b. Discerning
   c. Evaluative
   d. Appreciative

81. Which of the following is NOT a formal group?
   a. Command
   b. Task
   c. Interest
   d. Affinity

82. A ______ is a desired future state of an organization.
   a. Mission
   b. Value
   c. Vision
   d. Goal

83. The tendency to take more credit for successes than failures.
   a. Fundamental attribution bias
   b. Self-serving bias
   c. Causal attribution bias
   d. Self-efficacy bias

84. A behavior modification tactic that reinforces behaviors that are closer to the changed desired behavior.
   a. Framing
   b. Shaping
   c. Fixed-ratio reinforcement
   d. Extinction

85. Which negotiation strategy will likely be resented by one party?
   a. Integrative
   b. Distributive
   c. Mediated
   d. None of the above

86. View that all conflict is bad:
   a. Traditional
   b. Human relations
   c. Interactionist
   d. Devil's advocate

87. Which organizational design concept violates unity of command?
   a. Simple structure
   b. Bureaucracy
   c. Matrix
   d. Mechanistic

88. Type of conflict that is nearly always dysfunctional:
   a. Relationship
   b. Task
   c. Process
   d. All of the above

89. Which layer of the organizational culture is dress code?
   a. Observable artifacts
   b. Espoused values
   c. Enacted values
   d. Basic assumptions

90. Which of the following is not a method that someone tries to relieve cognitive dissonance?
   a. Change attitude
   b. Belittle the importance of the inconsistent behavior
   c. Rationalize away the dissonance
   d. They are all methods to relieve dissonance

91. Which generational cohort is most loyal to their employers?
   a. Baby Boomers
   b. Veterans
   c. Generation Xers
   d. Nexters

92. The model of learning that focuses on observation and experience is _______.
   a. Classical conditioning
   b. Operant conditioning
   c. Social learning
   d. None of the above

93. _____ is a decision-making style that is most concerned with personnel development.
   a. Analytical
   b. Conceptual
   c. Directive
   d. Behavioral

94. The reinforcement schedule of bi-weekly paychecks
   a. Fixed-interval
   b. Fixed-ratio
   c. Variable-interval
   d. Variable-ratio

95. A common disadvantage to group decision-making is:

a. Different perspectives
b. Training
c. Social pressure to conform
d. Knowledge level

96. Which is NOT true about the organizational development?

a. Seeks to make quick and radical changes
b. Value loaded to provide better services
c. Process oriented
d. Researches practical implications

97. ________ is an example of an external pressure for change.

a. Job satisfaction
b. Technological advancements
c. Productivity issues
d. High turnover

98. The factors influencing an organization structure decision are:

a. Strategy, environment and technology
b. Strategy, uncertainty, technology
c. Efficiency, environment, technology
d. None of the above

99. Communication channel with a central figure.

a. All-channel
b. Wheel
c. Grapevine
d. Chain

100. Technique good for ideas, but not for decisions.

a. Brainstorming
b. Nominal group technique
c. Delphi
d. Computer-aided

Answer Key

1. C. Power distance is the degree people can accept inequality.

2. B. Avoiding is when an issue is not worth addressing.

3. A. Competing is the use of assertiveness.

4. D. Accommodating is when someone knows they are wrong or the issue is unimportant.

5. C. Compromising is used when both parties have equal power.

6. A. Escalating commitment is continuous investment in a poor decision.

7. B. Negative reinforcement is removing unpleasant stimuli with a desired behavior.

8. B. Theory X and Theory Y assume that people are either very lazy or have the ability to self-direct.

9. C. Two-Factor Theory involves hygiene/motivator factors.

10. A. ERG Theory focuses on existence/relatedness/growth.

11. D. Equity Theory focuses on perceived fairness.

12. D. Learning organizations value risks and creativity.

13. C. Task identity is the degree an employee performs a job beginning to end.

14. A. Social loafing is the tendency for people to apply themselves less in groups.

15. B. Analytical decision styles rely on significant data.

16. A. Storming is characterized by conflict.

17. D. Performing is characterized by focusing on the task.

18. C. Forming is characterized by introduction.

19. B. Norming is characterized by harmony.

20. D. Satisficing is a "good enough" approach.

21. D. Expert power is based on skill or knowledge.

22. C. Coercive power is based on manager's authority to punish.

23. A. Legitimate power is based on the structure of the organization based on position.

24. B. Reward power is based on power to give rewards.

25. B. Mediation is third-party involvement to facilitate agreement.

26. C. The achievement-oriented leadership expects the most.

27. D. An entrepreneur is a top-level manager assigned to find and acquire business.

28. C. A spokesperson would represent the company publicly.

29. A. A leader is an empowering visionary and decision-maker.

30. B. The negotiator handles mergers and acquisitions.

31. A. The difference between where an organizational is and where they want to be is the performance gap.

32. D. Unity of command is each employee reports to one manager.

33. D. Self-actualization is the top Maslow need.

34. A. The five personality factors are extraversion, agreeableness, conscientiousness, emotional stability and openness to experience.

35. C. Expatriates live in a different country than their own.

36. A. Punishment is unpleasant stimuli for undesired behavior.

37. A. Machiavellianism is doing all necessary to get to the top.

38. C. Whistle-blowing is an employee's revelation of unethical or illegal practices in their workplace.

39. B. Maslow's Hierarchy of Needs involves physiological, safety, belonging, self-esteem and self-actualization.

40. C. Goals should have set times.

41. A. An intrinsic reward is doing a job because of like.

42. A. The traditional school of thought focuses on economic rewards to motivate performance.

43. C. The halo effect is rating someone based on a few attributes.

44. B. Eustress is a good stress that strives people to accomplish.

45. D. The Equity Theory studies perceived fairness.

46. D. Maslow's Hierarchy of Needs is topped with transcenders.

47. C. Mediation employs a neutral party.

48. A. Open-door policy settles issues in any management level.

49. B. Ombudsmen are employees that are sought for counsel.

50. D. The step-review system resolves issues with successive higher levels of management.

51. B. Utilitarian ethics base decisions on the greatest good for the greatest number.

52. B. Anchoring bias is the influence of the first information.

53. C. Job rotation is transferring employees to different jobs.

54. D. Job enrichment using motivators to increase job happiness.

55. A. Job simplification is the improvement of efficiency in a job (typically met with resistance).

56. B. Job enlargement makes a job more complex.

57. C. A monetary bonus is a positive reinforcement.

58. D. Extinction is the withdrawal of a reward.

59. B. Negative reinforcement is the removal of something unpleasant with a desired behavior.

60. A. Punishment is an unpleasant stimuli for an undesired behavior.

61. D. Task significance is the degree that an employee perceives the importance of their job.

62. C. Moral-rights are ethics based on a person's right of consent, privacy, conscience, due process and life.

63. B. Lowering productivity is changing inputs.

64. A. Internal locus of control people are usually more ethical.

65. A. Working conditions and pay qualify as hygiene factors.

66. B. Transformational leaders recognize employee needs and look at new ways to solve problems.

67. D. Charismatic leaders motivate and inspire; less predictable.

68. C. Servant leaders place others' needs over their own.

69. A. Transactional leaders are job oriented; less emphasis on personal.

70. A. Selective perception is processing only information that aligns with beliefs.

71. C. Collegial leadership encourages common purposes with strong focus on teamwork.

72. D. Leadership skills include technical, human and conceptual.

73. C. Groupshift is a when a group assumes more risk.

74. C. Goals should be specific.

75. B. Justice ethics stress the impartiality of decisions.

76. A. Incubation is the unconscious thinking about a problem.

77. C. Bureaucracies are most common in large organizations with routine tasks.

78. D. Organizational culture is created with purposeful selection, indoctrination and role modeling.

79. D. Evaluation is not a step of Lewin's planned change model.

80. B. Discerning is a listening style focused on main points.

81. C. An interest group is an informal group.

82. C. A vision is a desired future state of an organization.

83. B. Self-serving bias accepts more credit for successes than failures.

84. B. Shaping is a behavior modification tactic that reinforces behaviors that are closer to the desired changed behavior.

85. B. Distributive negotiation is likely to be resented.

86. A. Traditional view of conflict assumes all conflict is bad.

87. C. Matrix organizations violate unity of command.

88. A. Relationship conflict is nearly always dysfunctional.

89. A. Dress code is considered observable artifacts.

90. D. Changing attitudes, belittling importance and rationalization are all ways to relieve cognitive dissonance.

91. B. The veteran cohort is most loyal to their employers.

92. C. Social focuses on observation and experience.

93. D. Behavioral decision-making focuses on personnel growth.

94. A. Bi-weekly paychecks are a fixed-interval reward schedule.

95. C. Social pressure to conform is common in group decisions.

96. A. Organizational development does not make quick and radical changes.

97. B. Technological advancement is an external pressure for change.

98. A. Strategy, environment and technology influence organizational structure choice.

99. B. The wheel communication has a central figure.

100. A. Brainstorming defers judgments, builds ideas and encourages creativity.

INDEX

28294695R00061

Made in the USA
Lexington, KY
13 December 2013